Misunderstood

Surviving Suicide, My Story

Paul Anthony

Misunderstood

Surviving Suicide, My Story

Paul Anthony

2025

First published by Misunderstood, 2025
Copyright © Paul Anthony, 2025
First edition

The names of some people have been changed in writing this book.

Cover design: Paul Anthony

ISBN 978-0-646-71922-1 (Print Copy)

Dedication

To my eldest son, who tragically lost his life to suicide.

Contents

Foreword

I met Paul nearly five years ago when we were both working as peer support workers in a suicide aftercare program. From the very beginning, I saw in him something extraordinary—a healer in the truest sense. Not just because of the work he did, but because of who he is. I have witnessed Paul meet people in their darkest, most vulnerable moments and gently help them find a way back towards the light. His presence, his kindness, his humour, and his willingness to be vulnerable—to be real—have touched more lives than he probably knows.

Paul has lived through more than most could imagine. Trauma after trauma, loss after loss—experiences that could have broken anyone. And for a time, they nearly did. The depth of pain that led Paul to try to end his life is something I understand. I have felt that same despair, that aching emptiness, that total absence of self-love. And yet, here he is—not just surviving, but speaking, sharing, and giving others a reason to keep going.

It breaks my heart to know how much Paul wanted to die. And it fills me with indescribable gratitude that he is still here. These *bonus* years, as we sometimes call them, are sacred. And in them, Paul has done what few are brave enough to do. He has taken the wreckage of his past and transformed it into a message of life, resilience and hope.

This book is a gift. It is not just Paul's story—it is a lifeline for those who are suffering. I have seen firsthand how his story, and even just his presence, has changed people. I know this book will have the same effect.

If you are someone who is struggling right now, please let me assure you: I promise there is life beyond the pain you are in. I know it might feel impossible, but there is hope. Where there is breath, there is hope. I have lost people I love—siblings and friends—to suicide. I have tried to leave this life myself. I can tell you with certainty: there are people who love you, and people who would be devastated if you were gone, even if you can't see it right now.

There is always another option. There is support. There is community. And there is a way through.

Let this book be your reminder.

Bec Bennett
Service Manager
Next Steps, Suicide Aftercare Program
Grand Pacific Health

Grand
Pacific
Health

Preface

For a while now, I have been trying to find ways I can share my mental health journey and ongoing recovery. By writing this book, I want to empower others and foster hope and ongoing recovery during their deepest and darkest moments.

I have attempted suicide many times. The last attempt caused me to be resuscitated and intubated in an induced coma.

Someone found me on the beach after an overdose of prescribed medications. I had been laying in a coma on the beach for three days. I gained a brain injury, permanent nerve damage to my arm and severe pressure injuries to my leg. Specialists told me I could never work or study again. Through determination, therapy and changing my mindset from constantly wanting to die to wanting to live, I have proven the specialists wrong.

I have completed a Certificate IV in Mental Health Peer Work and work part-time as a peer worker.

Many days are still a struggle for me because my short-term memory is limited, and my ability to retain new information is difficult.

I also have a limited concentration span and have constant pain and numbness in my lower left arm, wrist and thumb. I will have to live with this for the rest of my life. But hey, I am alive, and I am alive for a reason. I am alive to help and empower others to navigate through the *misunderstood* journey of living with mental illness, suicidal thoughts and suicide attempts.

By sharing my story, I offer insight into what it is like living with mental illness and an understanding of something that is often *misunderstood*.

I hope that my lived experience of navigating through my darkest times can give others hope and help them strive towards ongoing recovery.

My diagnosis

Over the years, I have had many correct and some incorrect diagnoses. My primary diagnosis, among many others, is bipolar II. I will have to live with this for the rest of my life. I can manage it well with medication and help from various specialists when needed.

Living with bipolar

To understand what it is like to live with bipolar, I want to explain what it is briefly.

Bipolar is a mental health condition that causes extreme mood swings. Most people will experience mood changes in response to different life events, and their moods may fluctuate up and down.

With bipolar, you can experience extreme moods of feeling very high and euphoric and feeling very low with depression. The lows can be extremely crippling and can lead to suicidal thoughts or suicide attempts.

There are two main types of bipolar disorder: bipolar I and bipolar II.

There is one major difference between them. A person with bipolar I experiences more intense and extended highs, called hypermania. A person with bipolar II experiences hypomania, where the highs are less intense.

A person with bipolar I may experience psychotic episodes, delusions and hallucinations that can lead to hospitalisation.

With bipolar II, experiencing hypomania means you have more energy and self-confidence, feel more creative, are more sociable, flirtatious, sexually active, and have faster thoughts and quicker actions. You may be more easily distracted, irritable, talk faster, and prone to risky behaviours like spending money and being argumentative. There may also be an increase in drinking more coffee and substance use like alcohol, smoking and drugs.

With a depressive episode, you can experience feeling sad, empty or hopeless, have low motivation and lose interest in activities. You may also sleep too much or too little, have low energy levels, feel worthless or guilty, and have trouble focusing. Other things that may be an issue include weight gain or loss, suicidal thoughts or suicide attempts.

I have experienced all of these through my mental health journey and living with bipolar disorder.

✦

I have heard people say many times not to define yourself by your mental illness, which I agree with. However, I also think it is important to know what your diagnosis is, as with some disorders, medications can change your life. Bipolar is one of these disorders.

Prologue

The best and worst day of my life

It was 15 October 2019. A date I will never forget.

I woke up to a beautiful day. There were only a few clouds in the sky. I could not have asked for a more perfect time to implement my plan. I had been planning this day for a while, but with more detail over the past two days. I felt a sense of serenity, calm and peacefulness. This was the day when all my pain and suffering were going to be taken away. I would no longer be a burden to my family, children, or loved ones.

I took a shower, put on my work clothes, and packed my bag with a change of clothes, medication and prescriptions. I was ready. My mind was calm, and there were no longer any racing thoughts. I hadn't felt this good for many years. Wow!

As I did each weekday, I got in my car and drove to the train station to catch the 6:10 am train. I parked my car where I always do and sat there for a while, taking everything in with the clear sky and the day's tranquillity. I changed into my favourite jeans, t-shirt, and jacket. I took a pen and paper from my bag and wrote four letters, one to each of my children and one to my mum. I told my kids how much I loved them and that they would grow into wonderful adults. I told them I was proud of what they had already achieved and that what was about to happen was not to hurt them. They were not a cause of it, as I loved them more than anything and was sorry. I left the letters in my car and headed off into town.

My first stop was to get my prescriptions filled. I already had enough to kill a large animal, but I wanted to triple it to be sure. After all, I didn't want to be a burden to my children and have them spoon-feed me for the rest of my life.

The second stop was a massage. I love a good massage, and I don't mean the one with a happy ending. After all, I was already on my way to a happy ending. Following the massage, I had something to eat—I think it was KFC or McDonald's. Shortly after, I headed to my destination, my favourite place in the world—the beach.

As I walked through town and along the beach, I passed people going for their morning walk or morning exercise. I smiled at them and said hello. I wanted to tell them I was about to solve all my problems and had found the perfect solution to what had been a nightmare. It took me an hour to reach my destination. It was a great relief when I got there, as I worried my conscious mind might make me turn back.

I was sitting between two dunes, looking out over the sand and sea with no clouds in the sky. It was postcard perfect. I took my phone out of my bag and took one last look at some photos of my beautiful children. They meant the world to me and still do. In my mind, I was doing them a favour by taking away their pain and misery of having to live with a father like me.

A father who had failed them. A father who could not find his way through the terrible depression and the ongoing pain of living with mental illness.

I turned my phone off and put it in my bag. I didn't want to change my mind or end up in the psychiatric ward. To me, this was the equivalent of being sent to jail. After taking in the beautiful sights for half an hour, I got a drink out of my bag and took the medication. I put my bag under my head and lay on my stomach.

I could feel something uncomfortable underneath me, like a stick or something. When I reached under to move the stick, it happened. I couldn't move. My left arm was under my stomach, and I couldn't get it out. I also couldn't move my head. I felt scared, and I tried to call out for help, but I couldn't move anything, including my tongue and mouth. My whole body became completely paralysed. That is the last thing I can remember before falling into a coma.

Chapter 1

The early years

To understand my mental health journey, I need to share my story, beginning with the early years. While my mental illness is hereditary, several events have contributed to some of my darkest moments. The last ten years have been the worst.

✦

I was born in 1970 in the suburb of Otahuhu, in Auckland, New Zealand.

My family came from an economically disadvantaged background. It was challenging, but we did the best we could. My mum was a beautiful person with an empathetic and caring nature, and she still is. I know little about my birth father, Robert. All I know is he lived with mental illness, either schizophrenia or bipolar I.

Robert spent much of his life in and out of mental institutions, some of them because of suicide attempts. In those days, people living with mental health issues were misunderstood. Doctors put patients in straitjackets, drilled probes into their brains, and confined them like animals in cages. Robert was well-known for running from challenging and uncomfortable situations. He did this for most of his life, which would have contributed to his trail of failed relationships.

When I was three months old, Robert and my uncle from Mum's side of the family walked to the local chemist to buy nappies. While Robert went into the chemist, my uncle waited patiently outside. Little did my uncle know that after Robert had gone into the chemist, he went straight out the back door and disappeared. I must have left a smelly turd in my nappy that bought on a bout of post-traumatic stress. Whatever it was, he was out of there. My mum found out months later that Robert was living in Australia.

Two years later, Robert returned to New Zealand and contacted my mother to make amends and start again from where they left off. But it was too late for that, as Mum had gone through too much hardship and turmoil. There was no way that she was going to take him back. Mum was now living with my nanna and grandad.

I never heard from Robert again until I was in my forties. I only met him once out of curiosity. The only thing we had in common was our DNA, which included a bipolar trail of self-destruction. Thanks for that.

✦

My mum and I struggled for the next nine years. Mum juggled work, babysitters, schooling and extreme financial hardship. For much of that time, we had to live with some of Mum's friends, my nana and my grandad. Living with the Adams family would have been better than living with my grandparents.

My nana, grandad, uncle and aunty Lauren are, or were, an interesting bunch, to say the least. I'm unsure if *interesting* is the right word but let me tell you a bit about them so you can understand.

My nana and grandad had an alcohol addiction and lived in a housing commission home. They never owned a car, which was a good thing. If they owned a car, they probably would have killed someone. Nana would drink a whole flagon of sherry in a day. She would start from when she got up in the morning until she went to bed at night and never left the kitchen. I don't know how she was still standing at the end of the day—maybe she had suction caps on her shoes. I remember Nana would slur her words, and I found it difficult to understand her as she was always drunk.

Sometimes, Nana would get quite angry and aggressive with me. So, I spent time locked in my bedroom, in the wardrobe, or was yelled at, especially when Mum was at work. I loved her, but she was a difficult person, and I don't have fond memories of her.

Grandad had little to do with Nana and spent his time in his armchair in the lounge room. He would only leave the house to place bets at the TAB betting agency or to get some alcohol. Back then, they had a wireless (radio) that he would listen to during horse racing. He was a serious gambler, so they never had any money as he gambled it away. Somehow, they always seemed to have enough money to pay for alcohol—funny that.

These days, when I hear horse racing on the radio or see it on television, it is torture. I would rather rip my eyes out than listen to horse racing. It is worse than fingernails on a blackboard.

Then there was Lauren, and she scared the hell out of me. She had an intellectual disability, which was known as intellectually handicapped back in those days. Lauren had the mind of a five-year-old and was obsessed with me. She would say my name out loud again and again until I paid attention to her. She would say the same thing repeatedly, such as, *you're looking good today, Paul,* or *I really like you, Paul.* It was nice at first, but it would go on all day. Nana would get angry if I didn't pay attention to her or spend time with her. Little did she know I was trying not to shit myself every time she came near me. Lauren would inappropriately put her arm around me or her hand on my leg. I know she wouldn't have known what she was doing was inappropriate, but I found it confronting and awkward as a young child.

My nana had one of those old-fashioned bright orange vinyl sofas in her kitchen. It was so bright that you needed sunglasses to even look at it. I am surprised that it didn't make Nana vomit from having to look at it in her hungover state. Oh, hang on, she didn't stop drinking long enough to have a hangover. Lauren would sit down so close to me on the sofa that she may as well have been on my knee. I would move along the sofa, and she would follow me until I fell off the end. I remember hiding outside or behind trees so she would leave me alone, and trust me, she would come looking. Let's say that I was lucky that I could climb trees.

As I got older, I felt sorry for Lauren, as she never had an education or any help with her disability. She would spend the day rolling a hanky into a tiny ball, and my nana would ignore her like she wasn't there. After Nana died from an alcohol related disease, it was too hard for my grandad to look after Lauren on his own. Shortly after, she entered full-time care, where she received the help she needed to live almost independently.

Now, eccentric is the best way to describe my uncle. I am the sort of person who accepts people for who they are and what they stand for. However, if there is one person who will embarrass you and make you want to hide under the nearest rock, it is my uncle. I have never worked out whether he tried to embarrass you intentionally or if it's just how he is. But no one has ever embarrassed me like that before. He was an eccentric man and strange to be around.

My uncle spent time with me when I was young and often took me to the movies. He once took me to *The Swarm,* a horror movie about killer bees. I am sure it was for a 15-plus audience, but he wouldn't have paid attention. Whenever there was a scary scene, he would hide under the seat and scream at the top of his voice. People in the movie theatre laughed at him. I was so embarrassed. He would do the same thing when it came to a comedy movie. Instead of screaming, he would laugh loudly, like a cackling witch. The people in the theatre would laugh more at him than at the movie itself. I could share more about my uncle, but I would have to write two books to cover it.

✦

I don't remember much about my early childhood. I blocked some of it and can't remember other things. There were many good times, but there were also many bad times, and I mean awful times. One thing about how our brain works is that we remember the bad things that happen more than the good.

I had many babysitters while Mum and I were living alone. It was the only way Mum could keep a job and raise a child at the same time. There was one babysitter that I don't have fond memories of. There are others, but this woman was the scariest of them all and has stuck in my memory.

She was a tall, dark-haired hippy who lived an alternative lifestyle in an old house that was quite dark inside. A strong, sweet smell was always wafting around the house that incense would occasionally mask. Later in life, I realised it was the smell of marijuana. When I was in my early teens and smoked pot for the first time, the smell reminded me of staying with that babysitter.

I don't think she liked me much, as she didn't treat me well. I remember hiding in one of her rooms by wrapping myself up in the net curtains, hoping she couldn't see me. Sometimes, I would hide in the wardrobe to escape her. Maybe that was my safe place after being locked in one by my nana. She was quite nasty to me and scared the hell out of me.

I think the only thing that got me through those horrible days was spending time with her daughter. She was a little older than me and pretty, and I remember having a crush on her. There was a large, dark forest across the road from the house, and we would sneak out and play there. We would get in trouble for sneaking out, but staying at the house would have earned worse treatment. Half the time, she was too high to realise we were gone.

One day, while playing in the forest, we came across an adult book showing different sexual positions. We were too young to know what we were looking at, but we took it back to the house anyway. Being young children, we found it fascinating. Geez, did we get in trouble when the babysitter saw the book. When I think about this babysitter, I have a strong feeling that more went on there than I can remember. It makes me sick to the stomach.

✦

I believe my mental illness started from quite a young age. For as long as I can remember, I didn't fit in. I have never really had *my tribe*. Like an alien, I felt different from everyone else. People would constantly say that I was sensitive and a dreamer. If I knew what I know now, I would say, *hey, I suffer from mental illness... get stuffed*.

I had trouble making new friends. When I did, I couldn't handle having more than one friend. This was because I would suffer from stress and anxiety about whether I was spending enough time with each of them. I often wondered if they talked about me when I wasn't there. If I hadn't heard from one of them, I thought I had done something wrong. I suffered a lot as a people pleaser from a young age, and having one friend to deal with was hard enough.

✦

When I was about seven years old, I had a friend, André, and we would often get into trouble. Mum and I were living in an area of Hamilton, New Zealand, that I would describe as a ghetto. There were lots of old, run-down flats surrounding a park. This is where I met André, and we became great friends, often hanging out together.

André and I used to play on the grounds around the units surrounding the park. One day, we found a big flax bush, a native bush in New Zealand. It was so big that we built a cool hut at the bottom of the flax bush. It was like our home away from home until the day that André brought some matches.

Fire is fascinating when you are a child. So, what did we do?

We built a fire inside our hut. The flax bush and everything around it were on fire within a few minutes. We didn't know how to put it out, so we ran away as fast as possible so nobody would know it was us. However, we didn't go too far as we wanted to watch the fire engines put out the fire. I would hate to think how much trouble we would have been in had we got caught.

André and I used to love having acorn wars. We would hide behind trees and peg acorns at each other. It hurt when the acorns hit you, but it was fun. After a while, it became boring, so we amped it up a bit, pegged acorns at passing cars, and then hid behind the trees. One day, André threw an acorn so hard that it smashed the front windscreen of a car. I remember the driver being so angry that he got out of his car and chased us. I had never been so frightened. We ran through properties and climbed over fences to get away. We ended up back at my place and thought we had lost him. Mum was home, and I can't quite remember if we told her, but there was a knock at the door. It was the driver, and he was furious. He asked Mum if she knew of two young kids who fit our description living in the unit block. Thankfully, Mum said no, and he went on his way.

✦

We were destitute when we lived in the ghetto. But Mum did well to put food on our plates and a roof over our heads. I remember, though, there was a time when Mum struggled to buy clothes for me. A lady in the downstairs flat with a daughter my age gave Mum some clothes. I remember being horrified that I had to wear pink underwear. It's funny to think about it now.

✦

I don't remember Mum having many boyfriends when I was younger. There is one I remember—his name was like a sandwich spread called Marmite. I used to think he was cool because he raced stock cars. I have vague memories of sitting on the side of the track and watching him race.

The only other boyfriend I can remember is Peter, who married my mum and adopted me when I was nine. He lived in a flat close to us. I remember when Mum and Peter started dating. Their bedroom door would often be closed, and I am glad now that I never knew why. The thought of your parents having sex is vomit-worthy. That was when I first felt threatened and abandoned. It had been just Mum and me for so long, and now a man was taking her away from me. I felt hurt and angry. I wanted to tell him to take a hike and leave my mum alone.

This was quite a difficult time. Not only had Mum told me my birth father left when I was a baby, but someone else was now taking my mum away. I feel these events contributed to my low self-esteem, lack of confidence and abandonment issues while growing up. Broken marriages weren't as common in the seventies as they are today. You used to get teased at school if you didn't have both parents.

✦

My feelings of abandonment have contributed a lot to the struggles I have had in keeping relationships over the years. In the past, I have rushed into things too quickly and have clung tightly to my partner because I feared losing them. I was also drawn towards anyone showing the slightest bit of interest in me, even if we were not suited to one another. Then, the people-pleasing issues came to the forefront, as you don't want to upset the other person by ending the relationship. I would also gravitate to people with drugs and alcohol, as I feel that is where I belong. Maybe my nana and grandad contributed to that. I have improved in relationships now and have learned more about how my mind works. You become wiser as you get older.

✦

Mum and Peter moved into a unit together in a nicer suburb of Hamilton with a nice-sized carport and backyard to play in. They ended up getting married, and Peter adopted me. My last name changed, which I wasn't happy with, as it felt like I was losing my identity, but I got used to it.

Soon after they married, Mum fell pregnant with my younger brother. It was difficult for me when my brother came along. With him being the biological child of the family, I continued to have abandonment issues. I felt like I wasn't part of the family anymore. As I got older, Peter would attend many of my sporting events, which was nice, but I always felt like I didn't belong.

✦

Not long after moving into the unit, I made a friend, Ryan, who lived on the same street. We spent nearly every minute of the day together. It was back when you were gone from the early morning hours until the sun went down.

Your parents did not know where you were, as they had no mobile phones to monitor you. Ryan would tell his mum that he was at my place, and I would tell my mum that I was at his place. Our only rule was that we had to be back home before dark. Just like with André, Ryan and I would get into a lot of trouble.

One thing we would do was walk to the local university up the street from us. We climbed the fire stairs of one of the four-story buildings and waited until someone was about to pass and drop water on them. It took perfect timing. We thought it was pretty funny until one day, we got caught. I remember one poor person who overheard us laughing. He yelled at us and started climbing the fire escape to catch us. Luckily, we jumped to the next fire escape, climbed down, and ran away. We were so high up that if we fell, we would have died for sure.

✦

There was an elderly couple who lived next door to us. They were wealthy and lived in a large house with an in-ground pool. They would let me swim in their pool, which was fun, especially since they had two beautiful daughters a few years older than me. When they weren't home, Ryan and I would jump off their roof, onto their trampoline, and into the pool. It was pretty dangerous, as the house was two stories high, but we decided it wasn't daring enough after a while. To ramp things up, we made parachutes from rubbish bags and jumped off the roof. We were lucky we didn't end up in the hospital.

One day, while they were on holiday, Ryan and I broke into their house and climbed in through their garage window. We were curious to see what their house looked like inside. While in the garage, we found lots of candles and decided to set them up and light them. We were lucky the house didn't burn down. I am pretty sure nobody found out it was us. Who knows, maybe I was a pyromaniac as a child, as I loved fire.

✦

Mum and Peter decided to build their own house rather than pay rent, so we moved to the other side of town. It was a relatively new area, surrounded by farms and new houses. The move mortified me because it separated me from my only friend and school. For a child with no self-esteem and no confidence, it was confronting. I feared going to a new school and making new friends. It had taken me a long time to feel comfortable in my current school. It was probably a common thing for children to change schools, but for me, the anxiety was extreme.

On the first day at my new school, my anxiety was at an all-time high. The anxiety stayed with me for some time, and I would pretend that I was sick so that I didn't have to go. I would rather stay in bed than attend school.

Chapter 2

The school years

I don't have many fond memories of school. There is a huge chunk that I can't remember at all. It's as if I wiped it from my memory. I remember a few happy times, but not many.

I cannot tell you anything about the years from kindy to year five, as I feel like I slept through the lot. In year six, I realised why I remembered nothing. According to the teachers, I was supposedly dreaming my way through school. My teachers told Mum that all I would do all day was dream. I remember coming out of one of the so-called dreams in year six with the teacher yelling at me. When they stopped yelling, I returned to the dream where I had left off. They didn't feel like dreams. It was like I had gone into another realm and separated myself from reality.

This should have been the first sign that there was something wrong with my mental health. Looking back, I realise I was disassociating, not dreaming, and was shutting myself off. This could have been how I was dealing with the pain. This is the pain of shyness, low self-esteem, lack of confidence, and the overwhelming feeling that I didn't fit in.

In a way, I am glad that my mental health didn't spiral out of control until later in life. In the 70s and 80s, little was known about mental health, and what they did know was incorrect. Who knows what the doctors and psychiatrists would have done with me back then.

✦

Towards the end of primary school, I had my first girlfriend. She was an attractive girl and had a twin sister. This worked out well for my best friend, Kyle, and me. He dated the other twin, making hanging out easier for us all.

The four of us used to do a lot of fun things together. We would spend most of the time up the road from my house. There were many intertwined trees— you could call them vines. We would lay there, cuddle and have kissing competitions. As young kids, we didn't know what an intimate kiss was, so it was mainly putting your lips together and holding your breath. The winner could hold their breath for the longest without passing out.

Kyle and I had some fun times with the twins, but eventually, it had to end as we were so young. It is rare for a relationship to last at such a young age. I remember vividly how the relationship ended, which was embarrassing when I look back now.

My girlfriend and I were standing on the balcony at her house, and we both needed to use the toilet. She decided she had the right to go first as it was her house, even though I was busting to go. I was walking up and down her deck, holding onto myself. As a young child, I never had a father figure who could advise me it was okay to use a tree. I couldn't hold on and wet my pants. I was so embarrassed and didn't know what to do. When my girlfriend came out, I was trying to hide what had happened, but that was impossible. She laughed at me, and I wanted to dive into the deepest hole I could find. I had to get out of there and ran as fast as I could to get home without being seen.

When I got home, I sneaked into my bedroom and put my pants in the rubbish bin to hide what had happened from my parents. The next time I saw her, she made fun of me, and I threw stones at her. I wasn't trying to hit her or hurt her; I was letting off some anger, as I was so embarrassed. The relationship ended right there and then. When Christmas came around, she sent my mum a card, which I'm sure was meant to make me feel bad. Kyle split up with the other twin not long after our relationship ended. This worked out well, as Kyle and I could hang out again, just the two of us.

✦

In the area I grew up in New Zealand, you attended three different school levels throughout your education. There was primary, years one to six; intermediate, years seven to eight; and high school, years nine to thirteen.

When I reached the intermediate level, my life changed a little. I became more in tune with what was happening around me and wasn't disassociating as much. I put that down to discovering athletics, which turned into an obsession and a place where I could hide from my mental health challenges.

Every year, our school hosted the athletic championships. Being new to athletics, I was confused about what to do and what was involved. I would listen to the other kids talking about the sport, how they belonged to athletic clubs, and how they competed in weekend sports. I overheard a few kids boasting about how good they were and how they would beat everyone in the school.

On the day of the athletic championships, the first event was the 100 metres. The teacher told me that when the gun went off, run as fast as possible to where the people were standing at the finish line. They would identify the winner as the first person to cross the line. I was so nervous that when the gun went off, I froze for a couple of seconds. Once I eventually started, I gained momentum and overtook all the other kids. I ran so fast that I beat them all by at least ten metres. The local athletic club kids were angry. This was the start of my athletic career.

I ended up being one of the best sprinters in New Zealand. The main events I competed in were 100, 200 and 400 metres. The 400 metres was my specialty, and I became well-known for this event. The 400m was quite a technical race. Most people would pace themselves for the first 200 metres and then give their all for the last 200 metres. I would run the first 200 metres at full pace, get my second wind and keep the same pace for the last

200 metres. I found the event easy and thoroughly enjoyed it. It helped with my self-esteem and confidence.

✦

While in intermediate school, I was selected to take part in the national school athletic championships known as the Colgate Games. All the top school athletes from around New Zealand would get together and compete. The games were eight hours from home, so we travelled by school bus and stayed at a local school near the track. My parents drove down in their car and stayed in a nearby hotel.

I suffered from severe anxiety and nervousness when I was competing. While at the games, I would ask my parents not to come and watch, even though they had travelled eight hours to watch me compete. So, they would hide where I couldn't see them.

I reached the 400 metre finals and had to run against the fastest 400 metre sprinter in New Zealand. As always, I would get my second wind in the last 200 metres and noticed nobody ahead of me. When I looked back after crossing the finish line, the next sprinter was at least fifteen metres behind me. For a minute, I thought I had kept running after a false start, but this wasn't the case. I had won the race. It was probably the best achievement in my life.

I became obsessed with athletics, even though it caused me much anxiety. It became a way for me to deal with the manic episodes that I experienced with what I now know was undiagnosed bipolar.

✦

I was quite a loner when I got to high school, as I had trouble making friends. Again, my self-esteem and confidence hit an all-time low, and I felt different from others. Although I didn't have many friends, other students respected me because I was the fastest sprinter in New Zealand for my age group. I won all the local, state and national athletic championships in high school.

I glided through high school academically, although I experienced dissociation and, again, the feeling of not fitting in. Most of the kids hung out in groups. I didn't feel good enough to join their groups and put everyone on a pedestal. I would never study through high school, but somehow, I passed all my exams.

Even though I didn't feel worthy and had trouble making new friends, my success as an athlete made me well-known. I would break all the school athletics records and regularly receive awards in assembly. With all the popularity, I still only made one friend, Kevin. He was a great friend, and we would spend a lot of time together, but he had a wild side.

Kevin was not interested in school, and I often skipped school and spent time at his place. We would sit around eating fish and chips, smoking and sometimes drinking. We got away with it for so long, but a teacher eventually caught us. She was scary and taught the army cadets. One day, she saw us leave the school grounds, and when we returned an hour later, she jumped out from behind a tree. I swear I nearly shit myself. She took us to the principal's office and threatened to suspend us. This didn't stop us. We just found better ways to get in and out of the school without getting caught.

A boy from our school lived a few houses away from Kevin, and he passionately hated this boy. I never knew why, but Kevin would bully him. He would use his tennis racket to hit fruit at this boy's house every day, and his father would look for us at Kevin's. We would hide behind furniture so he couldn't see us through the windows. Kevin also bullied him at school. I used to get blamed for the bullying, even though I tried to stop Kevin from doing it. I got blamed because I hung around with Kevin.

There were many times when Kevin and I would be called into the principal's office for bullying, even though I didn't bully anyone. Kevin denied he was a part of it, but he was my only friend, so I took the punishment for both of us. During high school, I spent my time hanging out with Kevin and doing athletics.

I became so obsessed with athletics that it wasn't healthy. The athletic track where I trained was on the other side of Hamilton. My parents couldn't drive to the track as much as I wanted, so I would ride my bike there, taking me over an hour. I would train for two or three hours and then ride my bike home. It was crazy, but again, it was my outlet for my hypomania. I had decided to be the fastest sprinter in the world. I know people set big goals like that, but mine was extreme.

I was fortunate to train with one of the best coaches and some of New Zealand's top sprinters across various age groups. Training under this coach was extreme, and he would push us to our limits. As part of our training, we would have to jump over hurdles at full height with one leg. Sometimes, we had to do what they call bounding, which is taking long jumping strides with someone on your back. We would also take off from the starting blocks with someone trying to hold us back with a rope tied around our waist. The worst part was the nonstop sprinting around the track until you collapsed. You would have to run the first 200 metres at fifty percent capacity. Then the next 200 metres at sixty percent, and so on, until you reach one hundred percent. Geez, did your body hurt afterwards.

✦

I made a few close friends while doing athletics, but I gravitated towards those who would get up to mischief and often got me into trouble. There was one friend I had made who smoked marijuana. I remember going to the movies with him and a couple of his friends. Before the movie, we went behind a shed and had a few joints. I was so stoned by the time I got into the movies. My coach sat in the seat in front of me and tried to talk to me, but I was too stoned to speak.

I couldn't remember anything about the movie or my coach being there. However, I remember my parents coming to pick us up from the movies. They were so paranoid that they could smell the pot on me, so I wound down the window, saying I was hot. It was the middle of winter and bloody freezing outside. I'm sure they knew I was stoned. It was at that time in my life that I developed a love affair with marijuana. Not only did it feel good, but it took away the ruminating and racing thoughts in my head. It also helped a little with my anxiety. The hardest part was keeping it a secret from my parents and others around me, but I got good at it after a while.

Chapter 3

Booze, drugs and rock 'n' roll

While living with my mum and Peter, I had two friends I hung out with; one a few doors up and one across the road. The three of us used to hang out often, and that was when we weren't fighting. As they say, two is company and three is a crowd. Living right next door to me was a guy named Grant, who would later be the perpetrator of my rape. He was a big pot smoker and had a greenhouse at the back of his property where he would grow huge marijuana plants.

Grant didn't get on with the neighbours on the other side. They would fight a lot. One day, after a big fight, his neighbours informed the police about his marijuana plants. Somehow, Grant found out that his neighbour had reported him to the police and did a runner. I saw him driving out of his property with floor-to-ceiling marijuana plants in his car, and that included the passenger seat. It is a wonder he could see out of the car. Luck was on his side that day. He had just turned out of his driveway when the police drove up the road from the other direction. It was a close call.

Grant and his wife were swingers, and he was known to get men around to have sex with his wife. That was until one day, his wife fell pregnant, and he ended up kicking her out. This was so wrong in many ways.

✦

Living next to Grant was an interesting family, the Joneses, or, should I say, a weird and deviant family. They were father and son. The son was older than me, and I am sure he lived with undiagnosed autism. Mum felt sorry for him as he had no friends and would hang out with his father. So, Mum asked if I could spend time with him and get to know him. Little did Mum know what the family was like.

They would spend most of the time working on their hot rods. Their language took a bit of getting used to, as they would swear like troopers. Every second word was a swear word, and they even named their dog *Wank*. When I asked them what they did for work, they told me they did panel beating, spray painting, and worked out of their garage. They were operating illegally, without registering as a business. Not only were they running an illegal business out of their garage, but they were also running a brothel out of their house. The father was a pimp when the girls had outcalls. One day, I visited them and could see they had animal porn on their television. It was disgusting. I couldn't get out of there quick enough.

There was one good thing about them being panel beaters and spray painters. When I had a serious car accident on the way to go surfing, they fixed my car for free. In return, they asked me to paint three life-size murals on their garage wall. One was a mural of two rock and rollers dancing, and the other was a mural of Elvis and a naked woman.

The car accident was a horrible experience and was quite traumatic. I had my car for a couple of weeks when I nearly had a head on crash with a gang member on his way to a funeral. I was going down a winding road in the country when I thought I heard a tie holding my surfboard on the roof come off. I turned around to see if my surfboard was still there. When I turned back around, the guy was on my side of the road. The guy swerved, but it was too late. I took out both his doors, ripped off my front guard, and pushed my bonnet up near the windscreen.

The guy was furious and came running towards me like he was going to kill me. He had tattoos on his face, which were quite scary in those days, and he belonged to a notorious New Zealand gang. I could see he was angry, and thankfully, he calmed down before he got to me. I think it was because he realised I was only a teenager.

Because nobody was there to witness the accident, it was my word against his about who was in the wrong. Nobody was going to argue with a gang member, and I had to pay to get his car fixed. I bumped into him a few months later at a local pub near where we used to go surfing. I was underage at the time, but somehow got away with buying alcohol. I was frightened when I saw him, and extra scared when he started walking towards me.

He ended up being quite pleasant and asked me to wait outside the pub, as he had something that he wanted to give me. He walked out with a crate of long-neck beer. I couldn't believe my luck. Later that day, while drinking the beers, I found an ounce of marijuana tucked away at the bottom of the crate. I guess it was his way of apologising for blaming me when he knew he was wrong.

✦

As strange as I found the Joneses, I spent time with them. They belonged to a local rock and roll dancing club, which was a big part of their lives. One evening, they asked me if I would like to attend the club with them. Out of curiosity, I went and loved it—the people were friendly, and the dancing was fun. It was also cool turning up at the club in a hot rod.

The upside or downside of attending the club was the amount of drinking involved. Most nights, I would end up quite drunk, which was my way of self-medicating, and it helped reduce my social anxiety. The club gave me a purpose in life, and I felt like I was part of a family. For the first time, I felt like I was somewhere I belonged. I thought I had found my tribe.

Initially, I would dance with many women, but eventually, I found a permanent dance partner. Because we danced together quite a lot, we got quite good at our dance routines and entered a couple of rock and roll dancing competitions.

The competitions were fun, but also came with anxiety. There was one competition where my dance partner and I decided to try a flip. I ended up dropping her on her head. Don't worry; she didn't get knocked out but ended up with a lovely bump and bruise. Funnily enough, we did no more competitions after that.

✦

I made a new friend, Jason, at the club, and we would often hang out together. Jason was not a good person for me to hang out with, as he was into drugs in a big way. Being around drugs was a bad thing for me, as I loved the relief I got and had an addictive personality. I found that drugs eased my racing thoughts, anxiety and depression. It was another way of self-medicating, even though I didn't realise that until later in life. After all, I didn't know that I had a mental condition; I just thought I was different.

Jason and I spent a lot of time smoking marijuana and attended most of the club functions stoned. We tried different drugs together, including cocaine, ecstasy, uppers and downers, and even magic mushrooms. Jason used to get his drugs from some dubious suppliers, and I mean dubious. One day, Jason asked if I could give him a lift to score from one of his suppliers. He directed me to a rough area of town. We parked the car at the top of a hill and had to walk down a steep, dark, eerie driveway. I had only just started walking down the driveway when I felt something solid hit the back of my head. It was a shotgun. Yes, I had a shotgun held to the back of my head.

The guy holding the gun asked me who I was and what I was doing there. Jason knew the guy, but he hadn't seen Jason as it was dark. Thankfully, Jason piped up and said who he was, that I was safe and with him. They took the gun from the back of my head. I was lucky I didn't need to go to the toilet, or I would have shit myself on the spot.

There was a rather nice-looking, large, two-story house when we walked down the dark driveway. My nerves eased a little when I saw the house, but that was short-lived when I went inside. The house had no furniture except a table and a couple of chairs in the kitchen. Faeces covered the walls, and people lay everywhere, either on the floor or against the wall. Some of them had needles hanging out of their arms, and most of them were completely out of it. There was a girl who was lying on the floor with a baby next to her. She had a needle hanging out of her arm. I was scared shitless and wanted to get the hell out of there. My anxiety was through the roof. I already suffered from post-traumatic stress, and this was going to add to it.

Two scary-looking guys led Jason and me into the kitchen, where they sat us at the dining table. One guy sat down in front of me on the other side of the table and placed a gun on it. I seriously thought I was about to be executed. There was not much conversation between Jason and the two guys as they exchanged the money and drugs.

Before we could leave the table, the two guys put some magic mushrooms on the table. They said they wanted us to join them and have tea with the mushrooms mixed in. It felt like they would not let us leave without taking the mushrooms. So, I told them I had to drive my car and wouldn't be able to drive if I took the mushrooms. They seemed okay with that, wanting me to drive them into town. Initially, I thought I was only driving the two guys, but there were twelve people. There was not enough room for that many people in my car, but I was too scared to say no. They had to sit on each other, and one had to climb into the boot.

As we were driving through the middle of town, the police spotted us, put their sirens on, and pulled us over. Not only did we have too many people in the car, but the guys were prospects for a gang, and some had outstanding warrants. I was shitting myself. The other issue was that I had Jason's drugs in my car. I hid the drugs before hopping out of the car so that the police wouldn't find them.

The police ordered us to get out of the car and made us line up facing a wall with our hands above our heads. The police searched all of us and found some drugs. I was fortunate that they didn't search my car. I would have been in so much trouble if they had.

One police officer asked who the driver was, and I stated it was me. He looked me up and down and asked me to follow him around the corner. The officer asked if I knew these guys and what I was doing with them. I said that they were friends of a friend and that I was giving them a lift. The police officer took my details and lectured me about getting involved with these people. If he had known I was with them to buy drugs, he would have arrested me.

The police officer told me to get in my car and drive home. They suggested I not associate with these guys again. If I got caught with them again, I would be arrested.

They released Jason, and he avoided jail. I gave the drugs to Jason the next day. Unbeknown to me, when I took the drugs out of the car, a mushroom remained under the foot mat in the back seat.

My old car would leak when it rained, and my foot mats were always damp. Because of this, the mushrooms grew and multiplied under the mat in the back seat. One day, while cleaning out my car to put it up for sale, I noticed mushrooms had grown under that mat. I panicked, pulled out all the mushrooms, threw them in the bin, and scrubbed the floor as best I could so they wouldn't grow again.

A week later, I had another look to ensure I had got rid of all the mushrooms, as I had a buyer for the car. To my surprise, there were more mushrooms under the mat than before. Again, I got rid of them, hoping they wouldn't grow back. I'm sure the new owner would have found a stack of mushrooms had he ever lifted that mat.

✦

As time passed, I got to know more people at the rock and roll club. There was one couple I got to know well. John and Julie were about thirty years older than me, and we would spend some time drinking together.

John seemed like a nice guy, but that was until his wife caught him having an affair with a sixteen-year-old girl from the club. Because of the affair, Julie and John separated, and she threw him out of the house. About a month later,

I attended a club function that involved a lot of drinking late into the night. I spent most of the night dancing and drinking with Julie. We had so much fun, but it should have stopped there. Julie ended up asking me to go back to her place to continue. That was the worst thing I could have done. I ended up staying the night and sleeping with her.

In the morning, I got up and sat in the lounge in my underwear. While sitting there, I heard a car come into the driveway. The front door opened, and John looked at me from the hallway. He asked me what I was doing in his house this early in the morning. I had to think quickly and said I had come over to practice rock and roll the night before and had crashed on the lounge.

I knew he didn't believe me by the death stare that he was giving me. Julie walked out of the bedroom in only a short nightie with no underwear. A massive argument started between them just outside the front door. I could hear Julie telling John that we had slept together and that it was no business of his. *Great!* It was then I realised she was using me to get back at him for the affair.

Suddenly, I heard John go into the kitchen and open the cutlery drawer. He grabbed a knife, came out of the kitchen, and walked towards me.

This is crazy!

I grabbed my clothes and ran. John chased me to the front door. As I got about ten metres up the road, I heard him open the gate to let the dog out. I am not sure what type of dog it was, but it was scary and chased me, which took things to a new level. I thought I was going to get bitten. Luckily, the dog gave up the chase before it got to me.

I put on my clothes and ran as fast as I could. I headed to Mum and Peter's place, over a kilometre away. Unfortunately, John knew where I lived, so I had to get as far from my place as possible. It was Father's Day. I grabbed my present and threw it at Peter. I said if anyone came looking for me, he should say he didn't know where I was. There wasn't enough time to explain everything before I left. I didn't go back to the rock and roll club after that. The thought of getting stabbed was enough to make me stay far away.

Chapter 4

Bullying, rape and death threats

I struggled in year ten at school, not because it was too hard, but because I felt I didn't fit in. My only friend, Kevin, was leaving at the end of year ten and moving away for work. It was pretty daunting. I was about to lose my one and only friend and would have nobody. All I could imagine was sitting by myself during our breaks with everyone talking about me.

✦

Both Mum and Peter knew that school wasn't for me. Little did I know they had been searching for an apprenticeship so that I could leave school.

When I got home one afternoon, Mum and Peter sat me in the lounge. They said they had scheduled an interview for me with a sign company. I had never heard of sign-writing before. I knew I would soon find out when I attended the interview at the end of the week.

They said one prerequisite to being a sign-writer is being good at art. So, in preparing for the interview, I put together a portfolio of some artwork I had done in year ten.

The interview day came around fast, and I was nervous. This was my first job interview. I can remember shaking and wanting to vomit on my way there.

During the interview, I learned that sign-writing involved several types of tasks. These included designing, fabricating, and painting signs for displays, buildings, hoardings, cars, boats and other structures.

The boss and other staff who interviewed me were friendly and made me feel welcome. I wasn't confident, but the interview went better than expected. Towards the end of the interview, I showed them my artwork portfolio, hoping to make a good impression.

It was the best news when I landed the apprenticeship and was set to start in the new year. There were some conditions, though. With my year ten leaving certificate, I had to pass my art, English and mathematics subjects and obtain my driver's licence.

Because of my need to get out of school, I put my head down and easily passed my year ten certificate. After a few driving lessons with Peter, I got my driver's licence without any issues.

Getting your licence in those days was easy. You didn't have to go through the years of having a provisional licence. You only needed to complete a short written test, drive around the block, and do a parallel park to receive a full licence.

Looking back, I had imposter syndrome as I thought I was a terrible artist with no chance of being offered an apprenticeship.

✦

The new year came around fast. The interview was a walk in the park compared to my first day at the new job. I was absolutely shitting myself, and my anxiety was through the roof.

Am I going to be good enough? Are they going to like me as I'm not a likeable person?

My mind was racing.

The first few months on the job were challenging. For most of my life, I had my parents or a schoolteacher around to ask questions if I was confused or unsure. Now, as an apprentice, I had to learn to solve problems independently.

There was a guy named Gary, the senior sign-writer for the company. He was a bully and would contribute extensively to my mental health challenges in later years, especially my low self-esteem and lack of confidence. Gary was in his forties and was rather scary. He had eyes that would pierce your skin when he looked at you. I found him intimidating from the start.

Gary learned from a staff member that I was one of the fastest sprinters in my age group before joining the company. He asked if I would join his rugby team as he thought I would be an asset. I had badly injured my ankle, which made me give up sprinting a few months earlier. He wasn't too impressed when I told him I wasn't a big rugby fan and could no longer run.

Gary was obsessed with rugby and would spend hours talking with his friends about it on the work phone. The company owners would never criticise him, as he was a talented sign-writer and made them money. He could get away with anything. I knew little about rugby and didn't follow the game, apart from watching the *All Blacks* play. It was part and parcel of being a Kiwi.

I don't know what it is like being an apprentice today, but in the 80s and 90s, they gave you all the shit tasks. People pranked you constantly, and you were the butt of all the jokes. I didn't mind this so much as I didn't know any different and thought it was part of the job. There was one prank where they sent me to the local mechanic to get some elbow grease. They were angry when I returned with the grease we used for paintbrushes.

There was one day, though, when they were successful in pranking me. I had bought my first car, and while I was out on a job, they jacked it up and put it on blocks. When I tried to drive home, my car wouldn't move, and I thought my gearbox was stuffed. It was pretty funny when I realised what they had done.

As with any new job, the first couple of months can be daunting. In my case, it was about to turn into an absolute bloody nightmare. I had never experienced bullying, but I was about to face extreme victimisation. It was five years of absolute hell.

Things went downhill when Gary found out that I didn't like rugby and wouldn't play for his team. When I think back now, that was not the main reason for the bullying. I believe that he outright hated me. He was always nasty to me and refused to teach me how to do my job. He was supposed to be my mentor. In his eyes, I couldn't do anything properly. Gary would call me all the names under the sun and swear at me a lot. He would tell me I walked funny and spoke like a girl.

I remember one day when I tried to stand up to Gary. He had one of his rugby friends from his club come in for a visit. Gary told me to *go upstairs and make him a coffee*, using some very colourful swear words. This made me so angry that, for the first time, I stood up to him. I responded by saying I was busy with a job that I couldn't stop and that he shouldn't talk to me like that. He went crazy, and when his friend left, he said some nasty stuff and pushed past me, nearly sending me flying into some signs I had just painted. He was not reprimanded for his actions.

Through conversations I have had over the years, it was quite common back then for apprentices to be bullied. In the perpetrator's eyes, they were doing a prank or playing a joke, but it would often become more than that. They didn't care what they were doing to the developmental stage of a person's mind, confidence, and self-esteem.

This was when I had my first thoughts of suicide. I was downstairs in the computer room while everyone was upstairs having lunch. I was in tears.

How could I finish my apprenticeship when my supervisor hated me so much?

I thought something was wrong with me and that I was the problem. I felt like I didn't belong anywhere in this world.

I was so emotionally distressed that I immediately fell into a dark place. It was a place that I had never experienced. I didn't want to be alive. I walked into the factory and started looking for a way to end my life. While looking through my desk drawer, I found a razor blade where I kept all my sign-writing equipment. I went back into the computer room and started running the blade across my wrists to make them bleed. As I don't like pain, I couldn't go through with the fatal cuts.

Eventually, my boss came into the computer room and found me in a state of extreme distress. I quickly hid the shallow cut marks on my wrists. The boss took me into his office to find out what was going on. While my boss was talking to me, I had thoughts running through my head about what Gary would do to me. I thought about telling the boss that Gary was the one who was causing the extreme distress I was experiencing.

What would Gary do if the boss reprimanded him?

I knew the boss wouldn't get rid of him, and things would escalate. I told my boss that I was having problems at home with my mum to avoid the truth.

Being bullied by someone almost three times my age was a nightmare, and it went on for five long years. It contributed to my mental health challenges and was probably the start of living my life with imposter syndrome and hating myself.

I completed my apprenticeship as an inexperienced, unskilled sign-writer. After I left the company, I discovered I couldn't do half of what was expected of a qualified sign-writer.

✦

I spent some time with the Joneses and met many of their friends. Most of them were bikies, but two of their friends, Adam and Nat, would eventually become great friends of mine. They were a lovely couple; we got on like a house on fire. I felt like I had known them for years and would stay at their place a lot, especially after a huge drinking session. Eventually, they asked me if I would like to come and live at their place as a flatmate. I was excited about this.

The thought of leaving my family home for the first time in my life was daunting, but exciting at the same time. I would need to live independently, buy my food, and support myself. I could go out whenever I liked and come home late, even though I did that anyway.

Adam and Nat were extremely friendly and treated me as a good friend and with respect. There were only a couple of things that I could complain about while living there. One of them was when they were having sex. They were so loud that I turned up the television to block it out. It was also difficult to sleep some nights due to the noise. I am sure the neighbours from two blocks away would have heard them. The other thing that took a while to get used to is that they loved being naked.

They were nudists, along with Adam's brother and his wife. I remember cooking my first-ever meal and putting drumsticks in the oven when Nat walked past me and said *hi*. When I turned around to return the greeting, I realised she was completely naked. That was my introduction to nudism. It's awkward when you move into a house and find out you are living with nudists when you are not one yourself.

✦

While living with Adam and Nat, I would experience one of the worst traumas of my entire life. There are no words to describe what happened to me that night other than absolute terror. I would lock it away in the furthest region of my brain, never to be talked about for many years. Mum and Peter used to have a neighbour called Grant, the swinger I mentioned earlier. Grant was not only friends with my parents, but he was also friends with Adam and Nat.

Grant was an older, distinguished guy, not much younger than my parents. He was friendly, easy-going, and belonged to the same rock and roll dancing club I belonged to, but he had a dark side. I used to babysit his kids regularly. I would often see some of the guys that he brought home to have sex with his wife before kicking her out. It didn't take Grant long to hook up with another girl. She would become his new rock and roll dance partner and swinging partner.

One weekend, I was invited to a party at Grant's new house, along with Adam and Nat. There were many people from the rock and roll club at the party, and it started as a fun and boozy night. Only a few of us were left in the early morning hours—Adam and Nat, Grant and his new girlfriend, and me.

Eventually, Adam and Nat decided it was time to go home and asked if I wanted a lift. Before I could say anything, Grant told Adam I was having a good time and would give me a lift home. I thought nothing of it and was unaware of what he had planned. I trusted Grant as he was friends with my mum and Peter and was also good friends with Adam and Nat.

Grant, his girlfriend, and I sat at the table chatting and downing a few more beers. Everything was going fine until, slowly, things changed. After I had downed my last beer, I felt groggy and dizzy, and my body felt numb. My first thought was that I had too much to drink, and I was going to either pass out or vomit. This was a different feeling, a feeling that I had never felt. I didn't know it then, but my drink had been spiked.

I told Grant I wasn't feeling right, so he helped me from the table and walked me to his lounge. I flopped down on the lounge like a sack of spuds. Everything felt strange. My body felt paralysed, yet I could still feel all the sensations within my body. My mind was numb and groggy, but I could still understand what was going on around me. When I tried to talk to Grant, my words would come out back to front, like I was speaking in slow motion. I was getting quite scared.

When I looked over to the corner of the room at Grant, I noticed he was setting up a video camera on a tripod.

Why the hell was he setting up a video camera?

When I tried to ask Grant what he was doing, I couldn't get the words out; they were all jumbled. Suddenly, Grant's girlfriend was standing in front of me naked and started removing my clothes.

You might ask, why didn't you stop them? Why didn't you run?

I only knew a little of what was going on around me, and I could hardly speak or move. I was being drug raped. It took several weeks to remember everything that had happened, as it was a blur.

After Grant's girlfriend had her way with me on the lounge, they carried me into their bedroom and had sex with me against my will. Because I was drugged, I couldn't resist, yet I felt everything. They raped me.

When I woke up the following morning in their lounge, I was extremely sore in places where you shouldn't be—and I was bleeding. I knew something terrible had happened, but my memory of that moment was vague. I was in a lot of pain, but I found my way out the front door and ran to Adam and Nat's house.

I felt so ashamed of what had happened, and the last thing I wanted was for Adam and Nat to find out. I snuck into the house without them seeing me, went into my room, and shut the door. I cried for the rest of the day, night, and most of the next day and didn't leave my room. Adam and Nat must have thought that I had a massive hangover.

Because Grant raped me, I thought about whether this made me gay. I wondered if I would end up with a disease like AIDS that was going to kill me. Hey, maybe dying from some disease would be for the best. I didn't know how I would live with this for the rest of my life. I was too embarrassed and ashamed to share or report the pain and trauma of what had happened to me. I didn't share it with anyone. Not my family or friends, not my doctor, not my housemates, not the police, nobody. I would carry that trauma on my own for many years.

I never saw Grant after that, although I did see his girlfriend in town a few months later. She was across the road from me and ran when she saw me. It was probably a good thing she ran for her sake.

✦

There is a saying that things happen in threes.

Bullying, rape, and what next?

Another incident occurred while I was an apprentice for that sign company, and it will blow your mind. It also affected my trust in others, and I didn't think it could get any worse than it already was.

A big part of signage involves the fabrication and installation process, which usually requires two people. So, my boss hired someone specifically for the installation side, with me as the apprentice and handling the menial tasks.

The guy hired for the job, Troy, was a giant, standing well over six feet tall with a solid build. He had arms on him like tree trunks, a wild beard and shaggy hair. He looked like he had just stepped out of a Viking movie. Troy and I worked together on many sign installations and got to know each other. I thought I knew him well, but soon discovered I didn't know him.

While Troy and I installed some signs one day, we talked about our favourite bands. It turned out that we were both big fans of Pink Floyd. Their Auckland concert, a short drive away, prompted our trip, so we went together. A week before the concert, Troy invited me to his unit for a few drinks and to get to know one another better. The unit was in the same neighbourhood where I lived with my mum as a kid, the area I called *the ghetto*.

When I walked into Troy's unit, I noticed a massive picture of George Michael's face on the wall. When I say big, it took up the entire wall from floor to ceiling and the entire length of the lounge. Troy introduced me to two young ladies sitting at the kitchen table. I quietly asked him who his girlfriend was, and he whispered they were both his girlfriends. They all lived in the same unit and shared the same bed.

I remember having beers with Troy and his girlfriends, but the rest of the night was a blur. The next morning, I was in a different unit, lying in a stranger's bed in my underwear. I looked for my clothes, but they were nowhere to be seen.

What is this? Where am I? How did I get here? Where are my clothes? Who lives here?

I was scared and confused.

Finally, a woman I had never met came to the bedroom door. She told me I could find my clothes in the bathroom. I asked her what had happened the night before, and she said she didn't know. She thought someone had invited her to Troy's unit for a drink but couldn't remember anything afterwards. She had no idea who I was or how I ended up in her unit.

✦

The following Saturday, I drove to Troy's in my old MK1 Cortina to pick up him and his girlfriends for the Pink Floyd concert. On the way to the concert, Troy asked me to stop at a pub as he needed to go to the toilet. I hesitated to stop there, as it was known as a notorious hangout for gang members. When I pulled up, I saw that there must have been at least fifty Harleys parked out front. Troy was gone for quite some time. My anxiety was through the roof, thinking that the gang members might come out.

When Troy returned to the car, he asked me to drive to a phone booth near a service station twenty metres away. I thought he must have needed to make a call. However, he went to the back of the phone booth, where there was a window to the internal toilet of the service station. Troy had stashed some stolen goods in the service station window. He was now loading them into my car. Wow, I was now part of a robbery.

What should I do? Do I risk telling Troy that I don't want the stuff in my car and don't want to be part of this? Do I drive away and hope we don't get caught?

I drove away, fearing what Troy might do to me if I challenged what he had done. We continued our drive to the concert and were lucky to get a parking space outside the main entry.

As far as I remember, the concert was great, although I was too stoned. Marijuana joints were being passed around from person to person. It made me feel like I was a part of one big family.

When we left the concert, a patched gang member was sitting on the bonnet of my car. He had a tattoo on his forehead and was a big guy. I was frightened and didn't know what to do, and my anxiety was extreme. I asked Troy what he suggested I do. He told me to get in the car, and he would sort it out.

Troy walked to the front of the car and sat on the bonnet next to the gang member. The next thing I saw was Troy handing over some money, and the gang member handed him a bag of white powder. Bloody hell. Not only was I involved in a robbery, but now a drug deal.

I was happy to drop Troy and his girlfriends' off at home. I didn't sleep that night. I must have laid there for at least a few hours, replaying it in my head. I was sure the police would arrest me as they had my car's number plate.

My first job on Monday was installing several signs on top of a shop fascia with Troy's help. Back then, there were no safety procedures in place for working on ladders, planks, railings, or using safety harnesses. We had to balance on a skinny piece of wood and hope we didn't fall off. This is while holding a heavy piece of metal, a drill, a screwdriver and screws in your mouth. There was a high risk of falling and seriously hurting yourself.

Once we installed some metal panels, Troy took a ten-minute break. When he came back, he was wobbly and unstable on his feet. At one point, he nearly fell off the plank and took me with him. So, I suggested we stop the installation as he was unsafe and would continue tomorrow. I presumed he must have taken a break so he could take some drugs he bought on the weekend.

While packing up the work ute, Troy made a call at a local phone booth. *There were no mobile phones in those days.* When he returned, he asked me if I would knock off his girlfriend for him and that he would give me one hundred dollars. At first, I thought he wanted me to have sex with her. Of course, I said no, but then he offered to give me five hundred dollars. It was then that I realised he wasn't asking me to have sex with her. He was asking me to kill her. I laughed, thinking it was a joke and that he was poking fun at me.

When we got back to the factory, Troy went home sick. I wondered whether he was joking about asking me to knock off his girlfriend or if he meant it.

Do I talk to my boss about it?

I decided it was a joke as nobody in their right mind would do that. I would live to regret that decision.

When I got to work the following day, there was no sign of Troy. I thought he must be sick, but now they want me to install these signs myself. Then there was a phone call, and my boss answered it. It was the police, and they were looking for Troy. They said that he had scalped his girlfriend and had beaten her so severely that she was in intensive care in the hospital. I felt sick to the stomach—he wasn't joking.

Then the phone rang again. My boss answered it, said it was for me and handed me the phone. Troy had put on a fake voice, so the boss didn't know it was him. He said that I was the only person who knew where he lived, and if I gave the police his address, he would kill me. The threat shook me. My boss worked out who was on the phone, as I was as white as a ghost. He asked me if that was Troy, and I said yes. I told my boss what happened, and that he had threatened my life if I let anyone know where he lived.

My boss was friends with the local police, so he asked me to tell him where Troy lived, and he would let his friend know. I was so anxious and confused about what to do. Here was a beautiful girl who had been nearly beaten to death, and I was the only one who knew where the perpetrator lived. I had to tell them where he was to protect her, but my life was also in danger.

What do I do?

My boss understood my predicament and took me to the local police station where his friend worked. The police officer sat me down and explained that they would arrest and jail him, and I wouldn't have to worry about my safety. He had a plastic bag with a blood-stained shirt in it. He told my boss and me that Troy had several convictions in England.

I despise domestic violence in any form. I decided I would rather risk my life than have this guy get away with what he had done to this beautiful girl. So,

I told them where he was living. When they went to arrest them, he had cut his wrists and ran away across some farm paddocks and hid in a hay barn. The police sent out the dogs and eventually located him.

I am not sure about what happened after his arrest. If my anxiety wasn't bad enough, this incident had sent my anxiety through the roof. For years to come, I was looking for him or anyone who looked slightly suspicious, whom he may have hired to kill me.

Three years after the incident, I bumped into Troy's girlfriend at my local shopping centre. She thanked me for what I had done and said she was doing well. To my surprise, she asked if I would like to go to her place for coffee. I was ecstatic that she was doing so well after all that had happened. I gave her a lift home and went inside for a cup of coffee. I must have only been there for ten minutes when there was a knock at the door. It was Troy.

What is this? Why is he not in jail?

I could hear the fear in her voice when she said it wasn't safe for me there. She quietly told me to head out the back door, jump the fence, and go through the neighbour's property to get to the road. I swear I must have flown over the fence and run faster than Usain Bolt.

My life was never the same after this. I constantly looked behind me and locked all my doors and windows. I never trusted the legal system again and didn't feel safe in the police's presence. My anxiety had reached an all-time high. I developed a severe case of obsessive compulsive disorder and would constantly check locks and other things. I never felt safe.

Chapter 5

Wrong directions

During my apprenticeship, I frequently went clubbing with one of my work colleagues. We would get drunk and stay out until the early morning hours. There were several nights when we stayed out so late that we went straight to work from the nightclub in a very drunk state. I don't know how we managed to avoid being caught. I am surprised the three pies I had for breakfast those mornings didn't give it away.

On one of our visits to the nightclubs, I would meet Kate, the mother of my late son, Jack. We were both quite drunk during our meeting and had nothing in common. The initial attraction was writing her phone number on a tissue with lipstick. It was exotic, romantic, weird, and questionable at the same time. Our relationship moved quickly. Before we knew it, we were living together and discussing marriage. Kate came from quite a wealthy and religious farming family. Her family owned so much farmland that you couldn't see where it started or ended.

At the start of our relationship, we frequently visited Kate's family at the farm. It was fun at first, as it was something new, but it got less enjoyable over time as I got to know her family. I never felt like I fit in. I don't know if it was a *me* issue or if I always felt insignificant around wealthy and intelligent people or those with a higher status.

Kate's father was proud, especially of his achievements, from being relatively poor to becoming a successful farmer. I didn't like him much, as I found him to be way too overconfident and arrogant. He would often talk to people about his wealth and success, giving the impression that he was better than everyone else. I may as well have been a turd floating in the toilet, as far as he was concerned.

One weekend, while we were visiting, Kate's father was going to his holiday home for maintenance. I wasn't surprised that he had a holiday home, but I was surprised when he asked me to go with him. We jumped into his work ute and headed towards the middle of his farm rather than the road. I thought we must have been picking something up to take with us. We pulled up outside what looked like a large hay barn, and he jumped out of the work ute and opened the doors. It turned out to be an aircraft hangar and inside was a Cessna aircraft. I realised we were flying to his holiday home, not driving.

I had never been in a small aircraft before. It feels like you are flying in a shoebox with wings. If you think the turbulence in a large aircraft is bad, try it on a small plane. The plane rattles like crazy, your head hits the roof, and you feel like you will fall out of the sky. The flight was a new experience, and I enjoyed it, especially when I got to take over the plane's controls a couple of times.

We arrived at the destination and landed on an airstrip so small that I thought we would end up in the sea. The airstrip was at the bottom of a large mountain, making it even more tricky and scary to land on. Once we landed, we taxied the plane to a large two-story house on the edge of the airstrip and parked it out front. I didn't see inside the holiday house as we jumped in an old-style car and headed to his second house a few blocks away. Oh, how the other half lives. It was a fun day with lots of new experiences. As for her father, he barely uttered three words.

✦

Kate and I hadn't lived together long before we got engaged and married. It was probably one of the worst things we could have done, as we were incompatible.

Kate came from quite a large religious family, so we had a traditional church wedding followed by a large reception. With Kate having such a large family, most of the guests were from her side. They had everyone from first to fifth cousins. There were friends they hadn't seen for many years. I guess it was good, in a way. My family was small in comparison. Between our families, we filled up the church and the reception tables. I was just glad that I wasn't footing the bill.

✦

I felt elated upon completing my apprenticeship. The five years of being bullied were going to stop. Finally, I was going to be able to get away. I would prove this guy wrong and show him that I am good at what I do and a decent person. I would be the greatest sign-writer, travel the world and make large amounts of money. In hindsight, it was probably my bipolar talking, and with my lack of training, this would never happen.

Kate and I made a rash decision to escape to Queensland, Australia, and see how we would go living in a warmer climate. It was exciting to be in a new country to explore, with new beaches, cities, and hopefully better wages than in New Zealand. At first, it was daunting to be in another country, but it was also fun to experience new things.

We initially stayed with Kate's brother in Brisbane. Now, there are many words I can use to describe the way I feel about this person, but I won't. Let's say that I thought Kate's father had tickets on himself, but this guy was next level. Anyway, I suppose he was nice enough to let us stay in his house, and his wife and kids treated us well.

Kate's brother had dropped out of school early, and she described him as the black sheep in her family. He was one of those people who turned his life around and worked his way up the corporate ladder to become quite successful. He was a terrible cheapskate, though. I remember him taking us to a pizza restaurant for dinner, taking a chicken bone from his pocket, and putting it into a pizza. He caused a scene over finding the bone, and as a result, all our meals were free.

After being in Brisbane for a few days, I called various sign companies to find a job. There didn't seem to be any sign-writer jobs around, not in Brisbane anyway, so I decided to look outside the local area. After a week of searching, I got an interview for a sign company in Maroochydore. It was a few hours north of Brisbane on the beautiful Sunshine Coast beaches. I was excited to have landed an interview but was shitting myself at the same time. I prepared by creating a considerable portfolio of my work before leaving New Zealand to help sell myself at interviews. It looked damn good.

The interview went well once I overcame the nervousness, and the manager was pleasant and approachable. It was my first interview since leaving my apprenticeship, and I got the job. The manager said he was looking forward to having me on board. He revealed he had worked with several New Zealand sign-writers over the years and was impressed with their quality of work.

The interview was on a Friday, and we agreed I would start on Monday. They had a huge backlog of work. It was my first job in Australia, and I wanted to make a good impression, so I arrived early. I had hoped my first day would be spent on orientation, getting to know my way around and understanding how the business operates. Unfortunately, it didn't turn out that way.

The manager took me to a table and showed me photos of a large building that needed sign-writing. He had roughly sketched on a piece of paper how he wanted the signage to look. The wording was thirty metres wide and was to start two metres from one end and finish two metres from the other. The lettering was high on the building, requiring an extension ladder on top of a fascia. This was a daunting situation for me, as I have a fear of heights. I know it is strange for a sign-writer to fear heights, but I dealt with this fear the best I could.

I briefly looked over the photos and asked the manager where I could find the equipment to make my *pounce*. He looked dumbfounded and asked what it was. I was confused about why he didn't know what a pounce was. I explained to him that you used a piece of paper to mark out the lettering from an overhead projector. You would then go over the outline with a spiked wheel, making holes in the paper. You stick the paper to the wall onsite and hit the holes with a stocking full of chalk dust. When the paper is removed, it leaves a chalk outline of the lettering.

The manager told me he had never heard of marking out lettering that way. He insisted I go to the site with a piece of chalk and a ruler and mark it by hand.

Sod off. How was I supposed to do this? It was thirty metres of signage, two metres in from one end and finished two metres in from the other end?

I could only work on one or two letters at a time. I couldn't exactly stand back to see if I had marked it out correctly. This was the stage in my short-lived career when I realised I had missed the important fundamental components of being a sign-writer. After five years of training and studying, I was deemed useless. The manager and I agreed I wasn't suitable for the position, so I left.

What the hell was I supposed to do now?

✦

Kate and I drove back to Brisbane to her brother's, which wasn't a very comfortable situation. I believe he thought that I didn't try hard enough, and I just walked away from a good opportunity. I was so depressed and anxious about what I was going to do now. My sign-writing career was over. I had no other qualifications and wanted to curl up and die.

After a few days, I managed to get myself back together and started working out how to move forward with this new situation. I started looking through job advertisements and found a company offering an adult apprenticeship in plastic fabrication. Wow, this could be my opportunity to be retrained and still have a career. I attended the job interview and thought it went well. After a week, I had heard nothing and felt I should try to find something else, as things were getting increasingly uncomfortable with Kate's brother. After a few days of ringing around, I found an assistant house painter's job and started the next day.

I attended my first day as a painter, and my initial task was assisting the spray painter in painting the lattice outside the house. My job was to hold up a sheet on the opposite side of the lattice, so the spray paint didn't go everywhere. After about an hour of holding the sheet, my arms were aching severely, and to make matters worse, it was over 40 degrees Celsius. I was struggling.

After a few hours, the boss said he would go to the shops for ice blocks to help us cool off. After he left, one of the other workers told me that the boss had lied to me, and it was not a full-time job. He had only hired me for a few days to finish the house within the required timeframe. I didn't know what to do with the information the worker gave me.

Do I confront the boss about it, or do I leave?

The decision was simple—run and hightail it out of there. I probably should have confronted the boss about it, but I don't do confrontation well. The scary part now was how I would tell Kate's brother after working at the job for only half a day.

Kate's brother's reaction wasn't as bad as I thought, but he wanted to have a go at the boss. I asked him not to and to leave it as is. To my demise, the boss called home. He told Kate's brother I had left the job for no reason, and they had some opportunities lined up for me. Kate's brother defended me using my side of the story. Of course, the boss denied everything.

Who was her brother to believe?

Well, not me. This was the last straw for Kate's brother, and things turned nasty. We had no choice but to move out.

We headed to the Gold Coast to look for work there. It was beautiful, with lovely beaches and, hopefully, more job opportunities. Because our money ran out, we stayed in a tent on a camping ground until we could find accommodation. The first night at the camping ground was terrible. It rained solidly all night, but luckily, I had set the tent up on a slight mound, and we didn't float away. When I got up to go to the toilet, it was like a moat surrounded the tent, but that wasn't concerning. When I unzipped the door to the tent, a cane toad jumped in. It was the biggest toad I had ever seen. It was certainly fun trying to get that out of the tent.

✦

Kate ended up landing a job relatively quickly. She was hired to sell expensive handbags to Japanese tourists because she spoke fluent Japanese. This allowed us to search for a rental. We found a rental unit on the thirteenth floor of a high-rise, which had amazing views of the hinterland and fit our budget. The unit had only one problem: it had no air conditioning. I lay naked on the balcony tiles most nights, as it was just too hot. The poor neighbours.

After several days in and out of job agencies and searching the newspapers, I found a courier driver's job. I called the number and was invited to an interview for the next day. In the morning, I dressed in my best clothes and headed off. I envisaged the interview in a large building with loads of courier vans. To my dismay, the address given to me was residential in a questionable location. I presumed the house belonged to the courier company manager, who was interviewing from home.

When I knocked on the door, a guy who looked like a biker greeted me. He wore a heavy metal t-shirt, ripped-up black jeans, long, unwashed hair and a long beard. At first, I thought I had gone to the wrong address until he welcomed me by name and invited me in. The house was quite messy inside. He asked me to sit in an armchair after he cleared it of clutter and rubbish. I sensed that something was wrong with the situation. He asked me a lot of questions about my employment history and sales experience.

How was being a courier driver related to sales?

After being there for about five minutes, there was a knock at the door. The door opened, and around half a dozen people walked in wearing leather jackets with gang patches. This felt like a setup.

Do I run now? Were they going to rob me, beat me, or even kill me?

After everyone had settled in the lounge, I was given several books to look at. They were books from a direct-selling company showcasing various products, including makeup and cleaning items. This was not a courier job. They were setting me up to become a direct seller for them. I was upset, angry, and frightened by this stage. I wanted to leave, but I felt like they wouldn't let me go. Two of the gang members were even blocking the door.

The safest option was to do the rest of the interview and agree to take the books with me to learn about the products. In a few days, I would return to explain everything. Eventually, they let me go, and I ran back to my unit, shaking and relieved that I had got out of there alive. Along the way, I disposed of the books and didn't answer my phone unless it came up with a number I knew. I was also cautious everywhere I went to avoid bumping into them.

✦

I spent a month looking for work before realising a lot of jobs were in the hospitality industry. As the Gold Coast is a popular tourist destination, I took a hospitality course to get more job opportunities. One course I found focused on bar work. It lasted two weeks and was reasonably priced. Learning something new to gain new skills and improve my job prospects was exciting.

The course was well run; it was fun, and I met some great people. Over the first few days, we focused on the legalities and fundamentals of hospitality work. Then came the making and creating of cocktails, which ended up being my downfall. Every cocktail we made had to be taste-tested. By the end of the day, I must have made and tasted at least twenty cocktails and was pissed. I had been riding a push bike to the course. On my third day, I had an accident because of how much I drank.

I should never have got onto the bike. About ten minutes into the ride home, I crashed headfirst into a light pole on the side of the road. For the next few days, I suffered from a severe headache. I wasn't sure if it was from hitting my head on the pole, a slight case of alcohol poisoning, or a combination of both. I called the facilitator to let them know what had happened, as I couldn't return to the course for a few days. He said I would have to start again as I would miss too much. I couldn't afford to redo the course, so I withdrew completely.

I struggled to find work, and Kate's job was not going well. So, we decided to head further south to Sydney. When we first got there, we stopped at Bondi Beach. Our friends from New Zealand told us this place is among the nicest and most popular beaches. Well, it didn't give me a good impression of Sydney. To me, it was like a concrete jungle. There were no sand dunes, just concrete walls and buildings. It was nothing like the stunning beaches of New Zealand. I found out later that there were some beautiful beaches close to Bondi.

Again, I found it difficult to find a job in Sydney. It probably had a lot to do with my low self-esteem and lack of confidence. My undiagnosed bipolar may have contributed to this. Kate and I decided things weren't working out for us in Australia, mainly because of my inability to find work. So, we cut our losses and moved back to New Zealand. I felt like an absolute failure returning there.

What were people going to think of me?

✦

Things improved for us when we moved back to New Zealand. We settled into a rental property in Hamilton, where my parents lived. I landed a job as a designer for a large printing company, which involved setting up signage for large organisations. It was quite a stressful job as the quality of the product had to be precise. But hey, it was a job, and I was thankful to have one.

We moved again after I had been working in the new job for a few months. There was a beach we regularly visited on the east coast of New Zealand. It was a sought-after place to live, with miles of beautiful golden beaches, and we loved it. There was a large mountain you could climb and walk around. Sitting at the bottom of the mountain were some natural hot springs to soak in. On the west side was a beautiful harbour and a port where cruise ships would enter. It was a lovely place. We found a fantastic rental only metres from the beach, and we would spend time there swimming and surfing, which was great.

Not long after moving to the coastal town, I found a job operating a computer for a medium-sized sign company. It seemed like a great workplace; the manager was pleasant, and I got on with the other staff. I felt like things were finally falling into place for me, but that didn't last. The pressure involved in completing the jobs was intense. The manager would come into my room and tell me I needed to work harder and faster. It didn't matter how hard I tried; I couldn't please him. I am not the sort of person to get angry easily, but he knew how to wind me up. He was a real jerk, and that is putting it nicely.

As mentioned, I don't engage in confrontations well and still struggle with them today. I am sure this is part of living with mental illness. I avoid it to the point where I can't handle things anymore and explode. Sometimes, I think that if I could talk it out with people and back myself, things would work out for the better.

The manager of this company intimidated me. He was such an angry man and would lose his shit at the drop of a hat. I felt I struggled to communicate my feelings to him in a way that he wouldn't explode. He put so much pressure on me I couldn't take it anymore. So, I told him to shove his job up his ass and walked out. He was screaming at me all the way to the car and shouted that I was fired. I told him it was too late to fire me as I quit.

After leaving that company, I received a phone call from one of their biggest clients asking me if I would work for them. I was excited and relieved to get a new job so quickly, and I felt it was karma for the way I had been treated.

✦

A great guy managed me in my new job. He was well-established as a pinstriper for all the local car dealers in the area, and with lots of car dealers, there was endless work. Part of my job involved designing new, stylish graphics for the cars, which worked well for me as I could utilise my creative abilities. He set me up in an office with a computer and a vinyl cutter machine. This machine cuts lettering and graphics out of thin plastic with self-adhesive backing. I worked for him for the next five years.

We had one of the funniest guys I had ever met working with us. He was so entertaining. One day, I walked past a sunglass shop at our local shopping mall, admiring all the awesome-looking glasses. I noticed that one mannequin resembled my workmate when it moved slightly. After a second take, I saw it was my workmate. He grabbed some sunglasses from the shop and climbed into the display area. I was crying with laughter. He ended up getting thrown out of the shop by security.

There was one other funny thing he did that I will never forget. My boss would host an end of year party at his house. He had a tall pine tree at the back of his property. My workmate decided to climb to the top of the pine tree and swing his way down from branch to branch like a monkey. Everyone was worried that he was going to hurt himself. When he reached the bottom, he sat back at the dinner table. He stuck his tongue out, exposing a live prey mantis on his tongue, moving side to side. People fell off their chairs in laughter. Such a comedian.

✦

Not long after moving to the east coast, Kate fell pregnant with Jack, my oldest son. Everything was going well until towards the end of the pregnancy, when complications happened. Jack was born a few weeks premature and had to stay in the hospital in an incubator until he was big enough to come home. He was so tiny.

As with many parents, adjusting to a new baby, especially a small and delicate one, took some time. He was the cutest little boy, and I loved him to bits. I had a beautiful son with whom I would teach, play sports, and share my love. Raising a child is a full-time job, so I reduced my surfing sessions to once or twice a week for a few hours per session. The fact that I was even surfing would cause arguments between Kate and me. Eventually, I had to surrender surfing to keep the peace.

✦

Three months after Jack was born, our marriage fell apart. Kate decided she didn't want to be married anymore and wanted to separate. When I asked why, she rattled off several minor issues, such as leaving the toothpaste cap off and other little things. I knew this wasn't the main reason she wanted to end the marriage, as these could have easily been fixed. We separated anyway, and I moved out of the rental. I didn't want to be one of those parents who walked away, especially after having that done to me by my birth father. I would try to see Jack daily. I loved him so much and feared losing him.

After a few weeks, Kate dropped a bombshell and moved in with an old friend near her sister's house. It turned out to be her ex-boyfriend. I later discovered they had been secretly talking and possibly seeing each other during our marriage. Before Jack was born, I noticed calls to a country town four hours away. I checked our phone bill and wondered why it was so expensive because of the calls made to this number. When I asked Kate who the phone number belonged to, she said it was her sister's number. When Kate moved away to live with her boyfriend, she gave me a phone number to keep in contact with Jack. It was the same number she said belonged to her sister.

I had to get my head around the fact that I had lost my marriage. My son, whom I loved dearly, had been taken four hours' drive away to be brought up by another man. It nearly destroyed me.

Things became financially stressful due to the need to travel so far to see Jack and the additional costs of living on my own. There was no way that I could afford to rent my property, and I soon realised that I would have to live with other people. I listed many advertisements for flatmates, as it was hard to find people who would accept my son staying with me every second weekend. It was a struggle. I considered myself a great flatmate, but some people found it hard having a crying baby or a toddler running around the house. I think I moved houses at least ten times in one year.

I missed my son, and only seeing him every two weeks was a real strain on my mental health. I was drinking and smoking marijuana, as well as surfing. I would even surf while I was stoned or drunk. I made a couple of friends after the marriage ended. One I used to surf with all the time, and one of his friends who would join us when we visited the pubs.

✦

Not long after Kate moved in with her boyfriend, I got a call from her to say they were moving to Japan to live. I nearly died.

How can you take my son to another country so that I will never see him again? Sod off!

As much as I couldn't afford it, I visited a lawyer. I had to stop her from taking my son to Japan, making it difficult to see my son.

I found a suitable lawyer who didn't like how men were treated when a marriage ended. She reviewed my case and believed she could help. I had kept a record of everything, which made things a lot easier for her. Thankfully, I stopped her from moving to Japan, and she agreed to meet me halfway when picking up Jack every second weekend. Something was finally going my way, and cared about what I was going through. I didn't know I had woken the dragon. I was about to find out how nasty somebody could get.

How could someone hate me so much and put me through so much hell?

✦

Everything started okay with the visits and went as per our agreement. I drove two hours each way on a Friday night to meet at the agreed location. I did the same on Sunday night when I dropped him off. It wasn't long, though, before things deteriorated. It started with her being late and then not turning up. She would always have an excuse, such as her car had broken down or Jack was too sick to travel. I often had to drive the entire four hours to her house, which meant an eight-hour drive on both Friday and Sunday nights. I wouldn't get home until some ungodly hour of the morning.

Jack would scream ninety per cent of the way, as he didn't like the drive. It was deafening and stressful. I would also have to stop regularly to clean up vomit and try to calm Jack down. It wasn't pleasant. This had quite an effect on my mental health, especially my anxiety. Often, she would turn up with no shoes for Jack and minimal clothing. Sometimes, he would just have the clothes on his back. I would have to buy him new shoes and clothes nearly every time I had him. She would also turn up with no nappies, just the one he wore. After this happened a couple of times, I kept a bag of nappies in my car.

The long drive was taxing for Jack, who would be quite distressed when we arrived home. This caused issues with my flatmates, as it would often be very late, and he would often cry. Just about every time I had Jack, he would be sick, and I would have to take him to the doctor. I may as well have pre-booked a doctor's appointment every two weeks.

My parents lived the same distance from where I picked Jack up as I did. So, after a while, I stayed with my parents on the weekends I had him. It was good for my parents, who also spent quality time with Jack. It saved them having to drive two hours every second weekend to come and see him.

✦

I knew I needed to change my lifestyle. So, I cut back on drugs and alcohol and looked after my health. I returned to Taekwondo, which I had been doing before my trip to Australia. It became a big part of my life, and I would train nearly every night of the week. It was a place where I could go when I was experiencing hypomania. I also released my anger by kicking and punching pads and sparring with other students.

I started Taekwondo in the first year of my apprenticeship to defend myself, be confident and feel safe around the guy who was bullying me. As with everything I do, I had to be the best at it and became obsessed with it. I even entered some full-contact tournaments, hoping to be a great fighter. These tournaments had no weight divisions; instead, they went by belt level. It was a great way to learn to fight people of different sizes.

I remember my first tournament. In my first fight, I broke a guy's jaw with what they call a roundhouse kick. I won the fight but felt bad because I dislike hurting people. But karma struck in the second fight, where I had to go up against a guy twice my size. In this fight, I suffered cracked ribs and lost.

I made a few close friends in the Taekwondo club, which was great as I am not good at making friends, especially keeping them. One of my close friends was my instructor, a guy named Adam. He was a big, solid Māori guy who was very strong and skilled in Taekwondo.

One day, Adam was doing repetitions on his bench press in his garage. He was making it look so easy, and he asked me to see how many repetitions I could do. I considered myself a reasonably strong guy, but I couldn't even move the bar a millimetre.

Adam had a friend, Megan, and the three of us often hung out. I guess you could call us the three musketeers, as we did everything together. We all did Taekwondo, went for runs, frequently visited the local pubs and bars and went on motorbike trips together. We would often stay at Adams' place as he had a larger house, so we all had our own bedrooms. It also saved on the cost of the taxi as we could split it three ways. We were all just friends, so there were no relationship issues to worry about.

✦

I was surprised to learn that Adam had a wife and an adult daughter, Sophie, who had lived in Australia for a considerable time. He had never mentioned them. Adam's wife and Sophie moved back to New Zealand because Sophie was pregnant and wanted to have her baby there and be near her parents.

Our escapades to the pub stopped as Adam wanted to spend more time with his wife and Sophie. However, as Adam and I had become friends, I often stayed at his house. I got to know his daughter Sophie and his wife very well. Adam's friendship with Megan ended, as his wife didn't feel comfortable having her around the house, which was understandable.

Chapter 6

New country, new challenges

As I was spending a lot of time at Adam's house, it didn't take long before I got close to his daughter, Sophie. She was wild, but had a beautiful soul, and we seemed to hit it off.

The friendship with Sophie quickly developed into a relationship.

Were we just good friends, or were we dating?

We had a strong connection, so it was hard to tell. When I wasn't working, we spent every minute together, so it was like a de facto relationship.

That Sophie was pregnant didn't bother me at all. The father still lived in Australia and wanted nothing to do with the child. So, I thought that if the relationship continued, I would happily raise the child as my own. I wasn't there for the birth of Sophie's child, but I heard there were no complications, and it was a quick birth.

Not long after the birth, Sophie's parents announced they were moving back to Australia to live. They asked Sophie to go with them so they could still be with their daughter and grandchild. Sophie asked if I wanted to come too.

✦

Things deteriorated even more with Kate, and she made it more and more difficult for me to have contact with Jack. When I called to talk to him on the phone, she said he was in bed, sick, or didn't want to talk to me. I was being pushed away and treated badly for trying to be a father. She didn't want me in his life. It was heartbreaking, and it was making me mentally ill. Eventually, it got to the stage where I couldn't handle it anymore. She had won. I couldn't fight the battle to see my son or be a father. I was beaten and had failed.

For years, I disliked parents who walked away from their children—I still do. I think it is terrible to walk away from your children. But I also understand that sometimes the parent has no choice, as the other party can make it difficult for them to see their kids.

Where do you draw the line? How long do you fight for? Do you keep fighting a battle that can't be won and hurt yourself, or even get to the point where you try to take your own life?

✦

After many tears and heartache, I decided that moving to Australia may be the break I needed. I could get my head around things and get away from the torture of not being able to see my son. In the long term, it made me more anxious and depressed and led to a lifelong feeling of guilt and abandonment towards my son. The son whom I loved so much.

I called Kate to discuss my decision to move to Australia. I thought she would rip my head off, but she seemed elated that I was going. She wouldn't have to keep pushing me away anymore; I was about to take myself away.

I told her I would fly Jack over to Australia as much as possible and return to visit him. I told her I would like my parents to take over the visiting rights she agreed to.

My parents weren't happy with me when I told them I was moving to Australia. They did not like Sophie and worried they would never see Jack again. They understood why I was leaving because they had seen how Kate treated me and how I was constantly pushed away. At the same time, they were worried that I wouldn't be able to see him anymore. We ended up having a huge argument, which sadly led to us not talking to each other for more than a year. I always thought of them, and it hurt to the bone. I also knew that the longer you don't talk to someone, the harder it is to get back in contact.

✦

Sophie and I moved to Australia and temporarily lived with her parents in Sydney. It was fun staying with her parents; they would have friends over for drinks and party late into the night. The alcohol became a way of drowning out the pain I was feeling because of the distance I had put between my parents and Jack. The constant parties and drinking were fun, but eventually, I had to look for work.

When I first came to Australia, I had to be a highly skilled tradesman to work in the sign industry, but this had changed. Computers had taken over. You no longer needed to be proficient with a brush and have an eye for marking out signage by hand. It helped me as I was good with computers and felt skilled enough to work in the industry again.

I must have been on a high when I applied for my first job. A position was advertised for a production manager at a sign company. I applied for it and somehow got the job. I don't know why I thought I could take on a management position. On my first day, they threw me completely in the deep end, with no introduction to the company or training. I was fumbling around without knowing what I was doing. The person who had resigned from the position had agreed to stay to train me, but he walked out the next day. To top it off, half of the workers I was supposed to oversee had also left the job.

I had three buses that needed graphics applied to them and were scheduled to be picked up at the end of the day. The lack of staff prevented us from finishing the buses on time, so the company's manager reprimanded me. Later that day, I learned that the business had gone into receivership and was attempting to complete the last few jobs it had left. The pressure was too much, and I left the job on the third day. Again, it made me question why I could not keep a job.

Why did I fall into jobs that I couldn't do, weren't qualified for, or where businesses were closing?

✦

Things were getting strained with Sophie's parents. It was getting crowded, with all of us living in one house, and I needed to find a job so we could move out. I found a job advertised for a sign-writer with a small sign company. He was a sole trader and needed another sign-writer to help with the workload. I got the job, and they hired me to run the computer and the vinyl cutter. To top it all off, he was a Kiwi. Yes, he was from New Zealand.

Maybe this could be the one job I would hold on to. My new boss and I got on well. We had a lot in common, and things just fell into place. So, Sophie and I started looking for a rental unit. It didn't take long before we found a nice unit in a pleasant location. With the help of Sophie's parents and the money we had left, we could move into the unit within a couple of weeks.

✦

Everything was going well in the new unit. I was happy and could see a future. With Sophie's parents' help, we got ourselves a cheap car. Life was good. But it was to be short-lived.

It was a Friday afternoon. I had finished work for the week and headed home for the weekend. While driving up the street towards our unit, I noticed an ambulance parked outside our unit block. As older people were living in the same block of units, I thought that maybe one of them had fallen or had a heart attack.

When I entered our unit, two paramedics attended to Sophie's daughter in the lounge room. Sophie was visibly distressed. Her daughter had pulled down a pot of boiling noodles from the stove. It spilled over the front of her body, her groin and one arm. She was severely burned and was screaming in pain.

The paramedics asked if Sophie could accompany her daughter to the hospital in the ambulance. Sophie was too distraught, so I ended up going. It wasn't pleasant, and they could do nothing to calm her down. They tried to get a cannula into her arm to administer some pain relief, but they couldn't find a vein.

When we got to the hospital, they rushed her into resuscitation. They again tried to get a cannula in, but they still had trouble, and there was blood everywhere. I looked at her arm and chest; her skin moved and bubbled. I had never seen a burn so severe. They asked me to leave the room so they could work on her.

Sophie's daughter was able to leave the hospital weeks later, but she had to wear special burn sleeves for quite some time. The doctors advised that the burns would not heal fully, and she was going to be scarred for the rest of her life.

✦

My work started going downhill shortly after the incident with Sophie's daughter. My boss put pressure on me and pushed me to work faster. Maybe I was a slow worker, as it seemed a common request. As I didn't handle pressure very well, it affected my mental health. He said I should be faster and more productive as a qualified sign-writer and got quite upset with me.

One day, he gave me a task that involved cutting out some vinyl lettering and applying it to a sign at the far end of the garage. I did what was asked and noticed he was visibly upset with me again. I asked him if I had done something wrong. He responded that on my way to the sign, I walked past some rubbish on the floor that I should have stopped to pick up.

My hands were full, and I could not pick up the rubbish. My boss was watching and criticising everything I did. I couldn't do this anymore. In a situation like this, I would normally run to avoid confrontation, but I thought it would be better to leave on good terms. I told my boss that I wasn't the right person for the job and that he would be better off finding someone else more qualified. He was pretty calm about it and let me go. No bad words were exchanged.

I was freaking out about what to do now. Again, I couldn't hold on to a job. I was under pressure to keep a rental and support three people. Sophie was calm and understanding of what had happened. We sat down and talked for a long time about our situation. Sophie decided to find a job in the hospitality industry to help us financially, while I tried to find another job. She ended up finding a job as a waitress in a nice restaurant, which solved the problem of being unable to pay our bills.

✦

Within a few weeks, I landed an interview with a large sign-making franchise. I didn't know what a franchise was. So, I researched it and discovered that it was like a chain of fast-food restaurants but providing signage.

I went the interview and met with a lovely Italian couple who had recently purchased the franchise. The couple had no experience in the sign industry, so they were excited to have a qualified sign-writer assist and train them. My first job was to teach them how to run the computer system, vinyl cutter and printer.

It took quite some time to teach them, as they had no experience in the signage industry. I spent the first few months doing all the design work while they watched and learned. After teaching them how to do the design work, they sent me into the factory to construct the signs and apply the graphics. I would also go out on jobs with the husband and install the signage when he wasn't doing the sales and marketing.

✦

The franchise was growing rapidly, and they were getting more clients. To my disappointment, I was not allowed to return to do the design work on the computer. It was the job the wife wanted to do, and she enjoyed that part of the job.

Unfortunately, graphic design is not something that you can learn overnight, and some signs would look very average. As a graphic designer, you should know how much space to leave around the lettering so your eyes can focus on it properly. When the wife did the designing, the lettering would go right to the edge of the sign, and it looked terrible. But she did her best.

After nearly a year of working with the company, I had an incident that would leave me unemployed once more. One day, when using a sharp scalpel to weed away some vinyl, I slipped, and the scalpel went deep into my middle finger. I removed it, but blood started spurting everywhere. I took a rag from nearby, wrapped my finger, and showed it to the husband. He got the first aid kit and put a bandage on my finger. After that, he said I should return to work as we had a few jobs to get through. I was surprised they didn't take me to the doctor or send me home.

When I woke up the following morning, I couldn't move my finger, which really hurt. I called my boss and told them I wasn't coming in for the day and had to see the doctor. They joked about it and said that it was only a minor cut and that they would see me tomorrow. I saw the doctor that day, who was concerned enough to send me to a specialist the same day. It turned out that my tendon had been severed, and it had to be operated on as soon as possible. I told the specialist I couldn't pay for it. He replied that worker's compensation would cover it, and the company's insurance would cover the costs.

The next day, I returned to work with a splint on my finger. I told my bosses that the tendon had been severed and that I had to have surgery as soon as possible. They didn't seem happy about it, especially when I said it was a workplace accident and their insurance would cover it. Their initial attempt to deny it was a surprise to me.

I worked the rest of that day with a splint on my finger; it was painful and awkward. Two days passed, and they still had done nothing about the insurance to cover the operation on my finger. They still had me working hard to get jobs out the door, even though they knew I was in pain.

After the fourth day, they still had not told me what was happening with the insurance. That day, the specialist called me, saying I needed the operation as soon as possible, or I would have problems with my finger and hand. I told the specialist what was going on with work, and he said his receptionist would find out what was happening. The specialist called me back to say that my employer hadn't contacted the insurance company and that they would get on to it. I was fuming. There was a chance of losing the use of my finger, so I confronted my employers, which turned into an argument. I ended up walking out and telling them to find another sign-writer.

One or two days later, I was booked in for the operation. They sewed my tendon back together, but I had to go through painful and intense hand therapy over the next six months.

✦

While working with the franchise company, Sophie and I moved closer to the beach. We were lucky enough to find a unit two streets back from one of the nicest beaches in south Sydney. It was on the second story of a block of units with a balcony. We felt like we were permanently on holiday.

Not long after the move to the new unit, the relationship between Sophie and I deteriorated. It wasn't so much related to my inability to hold down a job; it was because we only got together as friends with benefits. I thought we might get closer and form a relationship because we were raising her child, but that never really happened.

One night, Sophie invited one of her closest friends over for dinner. We all had a few drinks, and the night was quite relaxed. I went onto the balcony for a smoke, and when I returned inside, Sophie and her friend were making out on the lounge. I wasn't angry, as I could feel we had drifted apart. We chatted the next day and amicably decided to go our separate ways. I talked with the upstairs neighbour about my situation. She said she could do with a flatmate, so I moved in the following week. Sophie ended up moving back in with her parents.

My mental health deteriorated. I lost my job, my friend and a child I had been raising as my own. It was a dark time in my life, and I had some serious thoughts about taking my life. I couldn't even contact my parents as we weren't talking to each other. I had lost interest in all activities, felt worthless, and my self-confidence was low. I was in a mess.

✦

I was again looking for another job to pay rent and make ends meet. After applying for several jobs, I got a job as a computer operator and designer at a large sign company in Sydney. They specialised in supplying and installing a sign product that they were importing from overseas. They were the only distributor of this product in Australia. It was a fantastic product, and everything snapped together.

This was one of the most enjoyable jobs I have had. The other workers were friendly and down-to-earth, and the manager was friendly and helpful. He was the type who would help employees if they weren't doing their jobs well, rather than giving them a warning or firing them.

I stayed with the company for five years. My depression was under control, but I was still experiencing hypomania.

✦

Things were going well with my new flatmate, Sam. The only problem was that she had a violent and jealous boyfriend. Sam was a free spirit and seemed comfortable walking around the unit in her underwear. This would upset her boyfriend, which I could fully understand. I know I wouldn't want my girlfriend walking around the unit half-naked in front of her flatmate. There was absolutely nothing going on between Sam and me. Rather than talking about how he felt about the situation, the boyfriend would get quite angry and violent.

One day, things came to a head, and Sam and her boyfriend had a big fight in front of me. He called me all the names under the sun and even pushed me to start a fight. Having spent many years training in martial arts, I stayed calm and didn't retaliate. The boyfriend stormed out of the unit and nearly took the door off its hinges on his way out. There were big pot plants on each level within the stairwell, and he smashed every one of them on the way out. There were broken pots and dirt everywhere. Sam called the police, but he had gone by the time they arrived.

I couldn't stay in a situation like this. I didn't like violence, and it sent my anxiety through the roof. Sam ended up changing the locks on the door, but I was worried he would come back and cause more distress. Sam had a history of taking him back, so I started looking for another place to live. I couldn't afford to rent alone, so I looked for shared accommodation.

✦

Eventually, I found a place in Sydney with a lovely lady, Jane, who was around the same age as me. The house was old, but large and right on the edge of a river. It was closer to work, so there was a lot less driving, and I didn't need to get up so early in the morning.

I ended up going on a couple of dates while living there. I will never forget one date I went on. The girl was younger than me but seemed quite mature. I often visited her at her house as she had no transport to mine or we would meet in the community. We only saw each other for a couple of weeks when she became possessive. She would constantly call me and think I was seeing someone else if I didn't answer the phone. I felt smothered and ended it before things got out of hand.

I did the right thing and ended it face-to-face. This was a big thing for me as I didn't like confrontation and would have felt safer ending things via phone or email. She didn't take it well and started screaming at me, so I grabbed my stuff and headed out the door. She followed me to my car, screaming at me one minute and begging me to stay the next. I got in my car and started to drive away when she jumped on the bonnet and landed on her stomach near the windscreen. I asked her to get off, but she wouldn't move. I slowly drove forward a couple of metres, but she still wouldn't move. I ended up having to get out of the car and physically remove her before I could drive away. For several weeks, I received nasty emails until I blocked her.

✦

I was adamant that I would never date again, but that changed when I met Amy, my kids' mother. She was lovely, chatty, and, most importantly, not psycho. Amy and I went to a gourmet pizza restaurant for our first date. Although we didn't seem to share many similar interests, we got along very well. Amy and I hadn't been dating long before I moved in with her and her sister. Looking back, we probably should have dated much longer before moving in together, as it was perhaps too quick.

Amy's house was in a fantastic location overlooking the city. Things were going well as Amy and her sister shared the house. We would eat and drink together and then disappear to our rooms for the evening. It was enjoyable initially, but after a while, things became strained. Having a couple and a single person living together can be challenging.

Even though we ate together, we were all into different foods. We also realised we had different ideas about co-existing under the same roof. Amy and I moved out and got our own rental. We found a place quickly as we were both working full-time.

Things were going well in our relationship. It wasn't long after moving into our rental together that Amy fell pregnant with our first child.

Chapter 7

Start of the decline

It was roughly around the time that Amy was pregnant that my mental health slowly declined. No, it wasn't because of the pregnancy, as I always wanted more children and was ecstatic to have another child.

So, what led to the start of my decline in mental health?

I know that my mental health is partly associated with genetics because I have a biological father who lived with mental illness. I know that several events and traumas in my life may have contributed to my mental health challenges.

But why now? Why, in my thirties, was my mental health declining?

Mental health issues can hit you at any time in your life. Some people experience depression, anxiety and various types of mental illnesses when they are very young, and some experience it later in life. For me, I have lived with mental illness all my life, but it didn't come to the forefront until I hit my late thirties.

Several psychologists told me there must have been an event that triggered an episode, but that was not always the case. Sometimes, I would experience extreme lows and symptoms associated with mania for no reason at all. There didn't need to be a specific event. It would raise its ugly head out of nowhere.

✦

I knew I was different throughout the first forty years of my life. Sometimes, I didn't handle stressful situations well. I often ruminated about things, became extremely obsessed, and had significant highs and extreme lows. I would dissociate myself from situations and life. My friendships were hard to keep, and relationships were nearly impossible.

For me, living with mental health challenges was not noticeable until later in life. I knew something was different about me, but I thought it was common among others to think and feel like I did. However, as the years went on, I noticed that how I felt about things and reacted to situations was noticeably different from others.

The mental health system was going through a huge learning curve in my younger years. My mum said that if only she had known what she knows now, she would have tried to get me some help. It was probably good that she didn't, as I might have been locked up in a psychiatric ward for life. I could have more brain damage than what I have now because of the lack of mental health knowledge they had back then.

✦

I was never your typical male and still am not today. I don't seem to have a macho bone in my body, and I am much more emotional and sensitive than other males I know. I have never needed to prove my strength or status as a male. This has always made it hard for me to make friends with other males, especially the alpha male. I have always felt awkward and felt I didn't fit in.

I don't have the urge to be a macho man and compete with who has the biggest balls. Quite a few of my intimate relationships ended for no apparent reason. When I asked them why, they told me I was too nice. This would also happen to me on dating sites before the relationship started.

How can you be too nice? Do you want me to yell at you and beat you? Sod off!

Over the years, due to not being a macho man, I have questioned my sexuality.

Is there something wrong with me? Did all those years of living with Mum on our own without a male figure take away my manhood?

No, I don't think that there is anything wrong with me.

Apart from living with mental illness and being brought up with Mum on our own, it has not made me less of a man. I am a passive, laid-back, caring and empathetic person. I have found, though, that I have got on with females much better than males over the years. It is much easier to share my emotions and feelings with a female than with a male, and I don't feel awkward about it.

I have had some close female friends over the years. However, I found them hard to keep because of jealousy from my partners, or one party might have wanted to take the friendship further. Sometimes, it was the mere fact that I would push them away because of my mental illness, or they feared my mental illness.

✦

It was when I stopped my sports and other physical activities that I noticeably became depressed. Amy and I decided that seeing the doctor would be a good idea. The doctor agreed I was not doing well with my mental health, put me on antidepressants and referred me to my first-ever psychiatrist.

Why do I need a psychiatrist's appointment?

Only crazy people see a psychiatrist. I am not crazy; I am just sad. I was certain the doctor had made a mistake, but I booked the appointment anyway.

When I walked into the psychiatrist's practice, a lovely receptionist greeted me and handed me a clipboard with lots of paperwork to fill out. Wow, there was some personal stuff they wanted me to share. One question was, in the past four weeks, how often have you had thoughts about suicide? Of course, I didn't want to end my life.

Why would they ask me that?

I feel sad. Another question asked how often I felt I wasn't worth much as a person. The questions also included how often I overreacted to situations, how often I felt hopeless, and so on.

Hey guys, this is me on a good day. Isn't this how everyone feels?

Finally, my name was called out to see the psychiatrist. A short, well-spoken Chinese man greeted me. His voice was calming, and he relaxed me, but I was still scared of what would come. Unlike what you see in the movies, he didn't ask me to lie on a large leather lounge and close my eyes.

The psychiatrist asked me what had been going on in the last couple of weeks and what had led me to be referred. *I thought you had the referral, so why are you asking me?* He wanted my version of what was happening rather than relying on what the doctor had written. My appointment was for an hour, but when I looked at the clock for the one-hundredth time, we had talked for a couple of hours.

The psychiatrist asked me to take him through my entire life from as far back as I could remember to the present. We talked about my feelings of abandonment as a child and the pain of having to accept a new father figure. This led to the bullying, the rape, and the desire to be the best in the world at everything. We also talked about the highs and extreme lows, disrespect for money, hunger for sex, over-thinking, self-hate, low self-esteem, lack of confidence and black-and-white thinking.

It was one of the most confronting appointments I have ever had. Things came up I had never thought about. These things I had pushed away to the farthest part of my mind and never wanted to revisit.

Why the hell are these things affecting me now? Why have they suddenly raised their ugly head? Leave me alone... and go away!

The words that came out of the psychiatrist's mouth would have a significant effect on me. To my detriment, I could not accept, *Paul, you have bipolar.*

I have bloody what? Some illness from the North Pole. I have never been to the North Pole!

He explained what bipolar was. After I heard him say that it is quite a serious mental illness and that it is lifelong, my brain shut off. Everything from then on was a blur. Well, that was until I heard the word lithium, which was the medication he was prescribing to me. That was when I thought he had gone off the subject and we were talking about Superman. That was until I realised it was lithium, not kryptonite.

The appointment ended, and I was given a script for lithium and a referral to get my kidneys checked. This was because lithium is not good for your kidneys. The psychiatrist asked me to come back in six weeks for a checkup, and by the way, here is your bill for six hundred dollars.

Following the appointment, I returned to work the same day and didn't say a thing to anyone. I struggled to understand what happened, let alone share it with anyone else. I dreaded sharing the news with Amy, as we had another child on the way. We also had to deal with my diagnosis, which I had to live with for the rest of my life.

When I got home after work, I explained to Amy what had happened and my diagnosis. She was just as shocked as I was. We were relieved to find a reason for my feelings and happy that I was prescribed medication to help.

✦

My kidney tests came back quickly. When the doctor said my kidneys were in good shape, I drove to the chemist and got my prescription medication. The first couple of days of taking the medication were okay, and I didn't notice any significant changes. I wasn't expecting to, as I was told that it would take around five to six weeks before the medication would kick in. Well, that changed after the third day.

When I woke up on day three, I was groggy. It felt like I had been on a big night on the booze. I got up, showered, dressed, and headed off to work. It took me nearly an hour to get to work, most of which was on winding country roads.

From the time I left the house until I got to work, I was in a daze. I could not focus. I would have had an accident if I hadn't driven that road hundreds of times. It was like I was driving on autopilot.

As for work, I don't think my boss got anything productive out of me that day. Thankfully, other designers in the company covered for me.

After a week and a half of living in a daze and not remembering how I got to work, I gave the medication a miss. I stopped them without consulting my psychiatrist, which is one of the worst things you can do. After all, in my mind, I didn't have bipolar, and the psychiatrist didn't know what he was talking about.

✦

Life went on as usual. My job was going well, but I still felt unsettled. I got on with everyone and was consistently told I was an outstanding employee. With all my jobs to date, I thought I was a terrible worker, even when someone complimented me on my work.

I thought they were complimenting me because they were trying to be nice. This is quite common when living with imposter syndrome. Low self-esteem, no confidence and feeling like a fake are also symptoms related to bipolar. Well, that is when you are not experiencing a bout of mania or hypomania. If you are experiencing it, you think you are invincible and will be the greatest in the world at anything you do.

✦

I made a lot of bad decisions while experiencing bouts of hypomania. One bad decision I made was to start my own business.

I wasn't having much luck at keeping a job, so why not start my own business?

It was a bad idea as I had no money. I convinced everyone that I had found the ultimate business idea to make me and my family loads of money. We would be rich, buy a nice house and travel the world. Yeah right.

I had walked out of a relatively secure job and had done very little research as to what was required to make this business venture work.

Or would it work?

I should have started on the weekends to see if it was going to work while I had a regular wage coming in. But hey, I was on a bipolar mission.

The business was called *Liquid Labels,* which specialised in domed labels. They are printed self-adhesive vinyl stickers and feature a polyurethane topping poured on top, making them appear three-dimensional. I spent days designing a logo, brochures and a website. I purchased a printer, a doming machine, tables, shelves, dehumidifiers, and special doming fluid. I set my garage up to be airtight and dust-free. It cost thousands to set up, but hey, it would make me rich. Since I had no money, I had to take out a loan to pay for it.

What I didn't know at the time was that there were other companies out there doing the same thing. Their fully automated machines spat out hundreds of domed labels in minutes. This allowed these companies to charge a quarter of the price of what I could charge for the labels. I couldn't compete and got knocked back by every company I approached.

What had I done?

When I realised I had made a huge mistake because of my hypomanic episode, depression hit. I fell into a dark, deep hole that lasted about a month. But then the hypomania hit again. I could start my own sign business with all the equipment I had bought. After all, I was a qualified sign-writer and got to work designing logos and brochures. Once more, I thought I would conquer the world and become rich. I would sign up franchises all over Australia and make loads of money. Again, I failed, let my family down, and put us in financial hardship.

I had to accept my failure and return to being an employee to get us out of a difficult financial situation. Because I did not believe in my ability as a sign-writer, I tried something different that was still within the sign industry. I went into sales.

✦

A job was advertised for a salesperson to sell sign products to sign companies in Sydney. They were after someone with a sign-writing background and some knowledge of the company's product. I thought I would be a perfect fit for the position, even though I had no experience in sales. I also wasn't great at selling my domed labels.

The company owners were based in Brisbane, and they flew down to interview me. I always sold myself in an interview, which surprised me, considering I had low self-esteem and no self-confidence. I put it down to being a good liar, which was odd, as I always saw myself as a person who doesn't lie. They called me the next day to say I was successful.

On the first day of my new job, they flew me to Brisbane for product and sales training. I was excited as I loved flying and staying in hotels. I soon found out why they did the sales training. The product I was about to sell was unpopular among the sign companies based in New South Wales. I would offer self-adhesive vinyl for cutting out lettering and self-adhesive vinyl for wide-format printing.

I should have known the sign companies in Sydney wouldn't be interested, as I hadn't seen much of the product when I worked there. They avoided it like the plague, as they had been using other products for years and were loyal to their suppliers. On top of trying to sell a product that wasn't popular, I suffered from social anxiety and hated confrontation.

Why the hell did I think I was going to do sales?

If the potential client told me they weren't interested and put the product down, I would agree and leave rather than challenge them.

After my initial training, the company flew me back to Brisbane and provided me with a mobile phone, a company car, and business cards. This made me feel important, and I decided to give the job a go. As is my usual approach, I thought I would be the best salesman ever and change everyone's perception of the inferior product.

I returned to Sydney and started my first day as a salesman the following week. First, I sat in the office and made a spreadsheet of all the sign-writing companies in the Sydney area. With that done, I started calling them to make appointments. Everyone I called said they weren't interested, and some hung up on me, especially when I told them the product's name.

I tried a different approach and didn't mention the product to them. I just made an appointment to visit them. They would turn me away as they knew what the company sold. They had a product they were happy with and weren't interested. I wasn't getting anywhere, so I thought I would try another approach and do some *cold calling*. This meant I would turn up at the company, hoping they had time to see me and try to convince them the product was good. This didn't work either. I don't think I was ever let into a sign company. Many of the managers were nasty and would send me on my way.

Not only did I have problems with potential clients, but I was also getting hassled by the two other workers who packed and shipped the products. These workers were worried that they would lose their jobs due to the lack of sales. They had nothing to do during the day. They played pranks on me, such as putting huntsman spiders in my desk drawers, as they knew I feared spiders.

I was persistent and tried my hardest to make a sale, but after a few months, I was still unsuccessful. I knew the owners weren't happy with me, especially after setting me up and investing money.

The company sent the sales and marketing coach down to accompany me on the road. He soon realised I wasn't doing anything wrong. The sign-writing companies in Sydney weren't interested in the product or changing suppliers. He told me he was leaving the company to start his own business. This made me think he might have realised the product was hard to sell. The product seemed to sell well in Queensland, but the other suppliers in New South Wales had a strong hold on the market.

I felt worthless and hopeless, and I was down on myself. I had to get out and hand in my resignation. The company owners didn't argue or try to keep me there. I think they were glad to see me go. Again, I had to find another job.

Chapter 8

Marriage, mortgage, kids

Amy and I decided to get married, so I proposed at one of our favourite beach locations and got engaged. This was a short time from when we first met, probably too soon. But hey, we were in love and enjoyed each other's company. Time wasn't a factor.

Because Amy fell pregnant, we planned to have the wedding before the baby was born. Our wedding was held in a park near one of our favourite beaches. The reception was at a yacht club on the edge of the harbour. We also booked a cruise around the harbour. My parents and younger brother flew in from New Zealand, and my younger brother was my best man.

Before the wedding, my mother pulled me aside and asked if I was doing the right thing by getting married so quickly. She reminded me of what happened with my first marriage to Kate and how tragic that marriage turned out. She was concerned, as she didn't want to see me go through the same trauma. The wedding went without a hitch, and it was a fun day.

Following the wedding, we headed to Sydney to stay in a hotel for the night and then to the Gold Coast for a week. I can't say it was an exciting honeymoon. Amy got sick with her pregnancy and spent most of the time sleeping in bed. I aimlessly walked around the Gold Coast alone.

✦

Following the wedding, I landed a job as a head designer for a large sign company. I still had my highs and lows, but the highs were becoming more noticeable, mainly due to not having sport as a release.

Over the years, I have dealt with my high and low moods by immersing myself in my sports and becoming competitive and obsessed. I always had to be the best at everything I did. With athletics, I had to be the best in the country. With Taekwondo, I had to be the best fighter and train harder than anyone else.

Until 2002, I was still very active. I was running and doing martial arts. In 2002, Amy gave birth to our son, Nick, and raising children is a full-time job. I was still involved with my martial arts when Nick was born, which helped me channel my mania into something not risky or destructive.

Amy eventually asked me to stop, as she needed more help with Nick. So, I stopped my training altogether, which added to the decline of my mental health. Again, it is not having children that led to my decline, as I love my children more than anything in the world. It was the fact that I had nowhere to release my highs. Eventually, extreme depression intruded into my everyday life.

✦

Not long after stopping my martial arts training, I decided I would immerse myself in art to distract myself from my depression and anxiety. It was also a way to have an interest that wouldn't take me away from the home environment. I had been dabbling in art since I was a young child. It wasn't until this time that I realised I might do something with it. I also thought it could be a way to help with my mental health.

Because of my love of animals, I started with some wildlife paintings. I used a medium called soft pastel, like chalk, but with rich archival pigments. It is a beautiful medium to work with. The pastels came in a stick that looked like blackboard chalk and a pencil, suitable for detailed work.

For the next ten years, I spent much of my spare time painting animals, from meerkats to tigers and horses. It was therapeutic and reduced my stress and anxiety.

After building up a collection of paintings, I entered art competitions. As always, for me, it was to go big or go home. I entered my favourite painting of a tiger into the *BBC Wildlife Artist of the Year* competition. I didn't expect to get anywhere with my entry as I was competing with other artists worldwide.

I was shocked when I learned I had become a finalist. This started my addiction to art competitions, in which I won or placed. My work was also published in magazines, and I received invitations to judge international art competitions.

After much success, I investigated ways to make money from my art. It was tough to get into art galleries. If you got in, there would be a long wait, so I looked into ways of selling prints of my art online. While searching, I came across some agencies in America and Canada that licence your artwork to be sold as prints. I sent some photos of my artwork, and they took me on board. Before long, I ended up being one of their top-selling wildlife artists. I would only receive ten per cent of sales, although there was no limit to how many prints they could sell from one painting. It turned out to be more lucrative than selling a one-off original painting. I had one sale where an author wanted one of my paintings on the front of their novel. They paid the agency $30,000 for it. I only got $3,000, but that was okay.

From all the success with my art, you would think that I would consider myself a good, if not great, artist. This wasn't the case. My imposter syndrome told me I was a shit artist, and eventually, they were going to find faults in my work.

Imposter syndrome makes you doubt your abilities and feel like a fraud. When someone compliments you on your achievements or abilities, you feel undeserving and don't believe or accept what they say. I experience this in almost everything I do, especially with my art. It can be pretty debilitating.

✦

After moving house many times because owners mostly wanted to renovate their investment properties, Amy and I bought a house. Looking back, I now realise that it was one of the worst things we have done. We had no deposit and were only just making ends meet. Amy's mother thought it would be a good idea for us to own a house rather than pay someone else's mortgage. She was generous in lending us the deposit. I didn't want to buy a house at first, as it was a big commitment, and I wanted to keep renting. It was frightening to know that I would be in so much debt. It caused me anxiety every time I thought about it.

After looking at a few properties and considering how to renovate them, I was excited about buying a house. When renting, you couldn't put a hole in the wall to hang a picture without permission.

Who would have thought that something so trivial as placing a picture hook on the wall would be so exciting?

✦

We ended up buying a house quickly, and it was the second one we looked at. It was an older house in a good area with four bedrooms, upstairs and downstairs, on a large block of land with a pool. The pool was our biggest attraction, but it was costly and difficult to maintain, which contributed to the financial stress.

Not long after we bought our house, the interest rates went sky-high, so we couldn't even pay our mortgage. We only ended up paying the interest on the house. This was another stressful time that contributed to financial pressure and anxiety.

It would take me an hour to get to work, as we had moved an hour down the coast.

With all the stress of purchasing a house and the financial stress, my mental health spiralled, but it was my beautiful children who kept me going. Two years after Nick was born, we had Lily, and another two years later, we had

James. No words can express how much I love my kids; they mean the world to me. The love for them has helped me pull through some of my darkest times. It is funny how your children ask you who you love the most or who is your favourite. For me, they are all my favourites. I love all three of them with all my heart.

If only I could have wrapped them in cotton wool and protected them from having to watch the decline of my mental health.

✦

My new job was a little different from what I had experienced. It was fast-paced, as the business had several large contracts with very short deadlines.

Three owners ran the company, and all three would tender for new jobs, which brought in work. For someone who didn't handle stress well, it was not a good situation for me.

The company soon realised I was struggling with the workload and hired more designers. The problem was that most designers had little experience, couldn't handle the time pressure, and would resign after a very short time. This made my workload quite heavy, which caused stress and led to anxiety and depression. I doubted my ability to do my job and experienced low self-esteem, low confidence and had imposter syndrome.

Looking back, while working with this company, I was experiencing bipolar episodes. When I was experiencing mania, it would help me in my work, but the depressive states were crippling. It was tough to get out of bed and have a shower. I find it hard to explain to someone how bad bipolar depression is. It is the darkest depression you could ever experience. I don't think anyone can fully understand unless they experience it.

I was with the company for nearly six years. During that time, I received two pay raises, a petrol card, and a company car. Yet Amy and I were still struggling to make ends meet. The expenses were overwhelming and caused some arguments. Amy suggested I get another job on the side or find a higher-paying job. I struggled with one job and would constantly be stressed about our finances.

The company's principal owner was stern and liked to show their power and hierarchy. Sometimes, I would work on one of his projects and needed additional information to complete the job. I would knock on his door or call him on the phone, and he wouldn't answer. When I saw his door open, I would knock and stand there, waiting for him to acknowledge me. He often ignored me for five minutes before saying, *What do you want? I am busy.* Some people would walk away without concern, but it affected me and made me feel more worthless than I already was.

An incident while I was working for the company resulted in me being off work for a year. One of the new supervisors was a martial arts instructor. With my background in martial arts, we would swap many stories about our different training techniques.

One day, he came into my office and wanted to show me a new technique he was teaching. It involved twisting the wrist into an awkward position. I said I was too busy and asked to be shown at another time. However, he pulled my arm away from my computer mouse and put me in a wrist lock. Because I was sitting down in a chair, my body could not move with the motion, and he tore the cartilage in my wrist. I yelled in pain, and he told me not to be a girl.

The next day, I tried to take a casserole dish out of the oven and dropped it on the floor. Not only did it hurt, but I had no strength in my wrist. I ended up having an operation and extensive therapy. I couldn't return to work for a year as it was my prominent wrist that was damaged. The guy ended up getting fired.

✦

I didn't know it, but one of the staff members with whom I worked closely noticed my waves of hypomania and depression. It would have been noticeable either way. When I was on a high, I would get so much work done that I would bounce around the office. When I was experiencing a low, I was unproductive and would keep to myself. This staff member asked me if I had ever received a bipolar diagnosis, mentioning his daughter's similar experiences with highs and lows. Yeah, right, I have bipolar.

What the hell do you know about me?

As time passed and my workload increased, things became tense at home due to financial problems. I felt pressured to find another job or work longer to pay the bills. The pressure became unbearable.

✦

While sitting in my office one day, I felt like my brain would explode. I couldn't function, and my depression had hit an all-time low again. *Should I ring Amy? Should I talk to my boss?* I couldn't do either, and paralysis gripped me. I had never felt this bad. It felt like I was in a dark, deep hole I couldn't escape. It was like someone had turned the lights out, and I didn't want to live anymore.

I had to leave the building, so I grabbed my phone and ran to my car. I didn't tell anyone I was leaving and drove home. The problem was that I didn't want to go home either. I have never cried so much in my life. I didn't know what to do, as I was in severe emotional pain. This led to my first suicide attempt.

While driving home, my suicidal thoughts got more and more intense, to where I couldn't bear the pain for a minute longer. About ten kilometres from home, there was a mountain with many good tracks for bushwalkers and hikers. I thought that would be the perfect place to end my pain.

I parked my car at the top of the mountain and walked into the bush for an hour to avoid running into anyone. I found a place about ten metres off that track where nobody would see me.

The attempt on my life didn't work. I fell into a pile of tears on the ground.

What was I to do now?

I needed help.

But do I want help?

I wanted to die.

I couldn't think of anyone I could call who would understand what I was going through. I remembered I had my psychologist's mobile number, whom I had been seeing for the past few weeks. She was a lovely person and very understanding, so I called her. Thankfully, she answered straight away. After explaining what happened, she said she would call the police and the ambulance. This freaked me out. The last thing I wanted was to be escorted out of the bush by police and put into an ambulance. I told her I would rather die than have this happen, so I refused to give her my location.

The psychologist said she wouldn't call the police or ambulance if I went to the hospital and stayed on the phone with her. She said that she would meet me at the hospital. I can't remember how she talked me out of the bush, but I met her at the hospital. She sat in the emergency department with me until I saw the hospital's mental health team and psychiatrist.

It was probably one of the scariest times of my life, as, rather than having thoughts of suicide, I went through with an attempt. I was frightened beyond words.

What were they going to do with me now? Were they going to lock me up and throw away the key? Shit! Help?

It didn't take long before the mental health team and psychiatrist saw me. They said I needed to be in the hospital for a few weeks for my safety. They didn't want to put me in the psychiatric ward at the hospital where I was, as there were very sick and violent patients there. Luckily, I had private health insurance, and they could get me into a private mental health hospital the following day. I was extremely anxious and scared to go to the hospital, as I didn't know what to expect. I imagined myself in a straitjacket, heavily sedated with tranquilisers.

I was pleasantly surprised when I arrived at the private mental health hospital. A kind intake nurse greeted me, asked me to fill out some forms, and took me to my room. The room was huge and carpeted.

What more could you want than to stay in a resort?

Sadly, I was unable to appreciate the surroundings. After all, I had just made an attempt on my life.

Once I had put my bag in the room, the nurse showed me around the rest of the hospital, and again, I was pleasantly surprised. The hospital had a large courtyard with tables, deckchairs and bean bags. There was also a gym, an art room, and a dining room that looked like a restaurant, complete with a professional chef. There were therapy rooms where you had daily group meetings, and you worked on techniques such as cognitive behaviour and dialectical behaviour therapy.

✦

During my stay, I had my medication altered by the psychiatrist. He also gave me another medication, which sedated me a little.

When Amy visited me, I considered looking for another career that may give me more opportunities and a pay increase. I had plenty of time to look for new job prospects and career paths during my stay. I soon found an advertisement to train as an endorsed enrolled nurse. So, I applied for the position and got an interview within a week. I got a few hours' leave from the hospital to attend the interview, although I didn't tell them. I know they would have told me it was not a good idea with the state of my mental health. So, I told them I was walking into town and along the beach.

The interview was quite confronting as I sat in front of four interviewers. A couple of people were from Tertiary and Further Education (TAFE), and the others were from the hospital where I would do my placements. Luckily, I had taken some of my sedation medication a few hours before attending the interview. I was so relaxed that it wasn't funny. I had no nerves whatsoever and nailed the interview. The interviewers did not know that I was currently staying in a mental health hospital and had recently tried to take my life. A couple of days later, I got a call to say that I had landed the opportunity to train as a nurse.

✦

The hospital released me after three weeks, the standard length of stay. The psychiatrist made sure that I had psychologist appointments lined up and gave me scripts for my medications. Four weeks after I left the hospital, I started my diploma as an endorsed enrolled nurse. I was happy to resign from my position as a graphic designer at the sign company, as I found it too stressful.

While attending TAFE, I got a part-time nursing assistant position at a private hospital. I primarily worked night shifts to attend TAFE during the day. I experienced hypomania and insomnia, which made it easier to juggle work and study with almost no sleep.

Following my first suicide attempt and the three-week hospital stay, I tried my hardest to fit back into the real world again. I did the best I could to juggle study and work and everything I could to fight my depression and take control of my hypomania. It was challenging to do as mental illness had become a big part of my life, and I wasn't getting the treatment for my bipolar. It was only a matter of time before I fell back into that deep, dark hole of depression, with many more suicide attempts to come.

✦

While my children were growing up, they had amazing sporting abilities and could easily pick up any sport. Amy and I thought it would be good for our children to do sports to give them an interest and keep them grounded. Due to the challenges of juggling work and studies, we encouraged them to take part in the same sport. This was so we would only have to attend one venue and not drive all over the place.

T-ball was a sport that children started at a young age. They learned to hit a ball off a tee in this grassroots part of baseball. However, they wouldn't know what to do after they hit the ball and would run the wrong way.

The next stage of baseball for children was called Zooka. In this stage, the ball is shot out of a machine, but it is a little slower than the person pitching the ball. This was quite scary for children, and they often left the sport when they reached this level. My eldest son, Nick, got through one season of Zooka, but all three children decided they had enough and didn't want to do another season.

One of the other sports the children wanted to play was soccer. Nick was the first to play, as several friends played in different teams. My youngest two, James and Lily, played soccer around the same time, but played in the little children's league. The league wasn't competitive and used only a small part of the field. It was funny and cute to watch the children dribble the ball in the wrong direction and score at the wrong end of the field.

Nick did very well in his first season of soccer. His team ended up either winning or coming second. The boys kept their team together the following year, but there was one issue. The team coach didn't want to do another season, so the boys were left without a coach. One of the club's organisers invited all the players and parents to appoint another coach. None of the parents put their hand up to take over the role. I felt so bad for the children because they couldn't compete without a coach, so I volunteered for the job.

I had found something else to become obsessed with and decided that I would be the best coach ever. Hey, I was going to coach Manchester United. I even put myself through training courses that weren't required for my boys' level of soccer. I researched the Internet for soccer drills and activities to help the boys improve their skills as players. To Amy's disgust, I also bought training equipment, such as cones, balls, and pop-up goals. I was on a mission.

As much as I enjoyed being a coach, it caused much anxiety. One thing that added to my anxiety was that nobody in the team wanted to be the goalie. Everyone hated the position and would be upset with me if I assigned them the task. If the other team scored, the team would blame themselves or their teammates would hassle them. I am an empathetic person, and I would call myself an empath. If any of the children were distressed, I would feel their pain, which would upset me.

The boys ended up easily winning the season. No other teams had even come close to beating them. I could see the boys becoming bored, as their grades were too easy for them. So, I decided it was time to speak with the club organisers and get them moved up from second to first grade.

The following season was highly competitive, with the boys being moved up a grade. The games were close, and they lost quite a few. The boys got upset with losing, saying it wasn't fair and wanting to go back down a grade. This added to my anxiety, caused me stress, and led to depression. *Why did I put them up?* I am a terrible coach. My self-esteem and confidence as a coach went out the door.

I ended up finishing the season, but there was no way that I could carry on. My mental health had declined. The following season, the boys had to move to the next age group. The team was broken apart, and many boys gave up soccer altogether.

✦

Tennis was the next sport that my children got involved in. This sport would take over our lives, and we became a tennis family. We were told about a tennis camp held at the tennis courts near our home during the school holidays. This would be a great way to keep the children occupied and have some fun at the same time. The children loved the game and took to it like a duck to water.

Nick was the first one to excel at tennis. The head coach told us that Nick showed real talent during the tennis camp. He asked if Nick could come along and train with the club. This was quite exciting for Nick, as he had found something he enjoyed and excelled at. He started training with the club once a week and increased it to more days as he improved.

The son of the tennis camp's owner, a highly qualified Tennis New South Wales coach, trained Nick. The coach worked on growing Nick's talent and, after a while, encouraged him to compete in local tennis tournaments.

Nick started at the beginner's level and quickly worked his way up the rankings. He played at the top level of the local competition, which was called Davis Cup A. He became unbeatable in the local tennis competitions and created a name for himself.

We noticed Nick was getting bored with the local competition and needed a challenge, just as much as he loved winning. One parent in the local competition told us about the junior development series tournaments held most weekends at various locations. The tournaments catered to children who wanted to advance their tennis careers. We decided these tournaments would be perfect for Nick.

✦

As James and Lily got older, our local tennis club began to train and coach them, and like Nick, they showed talent. They entered the local competitions and slowly started climbing the rankings within the local area. Having their older brother Nick to hit with was a bonus. They gained the ability to receive and return balls at a fast speed, as well as receiving some quick serves.

We would spend most weekends hitting a ball at our local tennis courts. As there were four of us, we could play singles and doubles without one having to wait for a turn. It was a wonderful way to bond with my children, and we had a great deal of fun together.

✦

Nick quickly worked his way up the junior development series tournament rankings. It was a bit confronting for him at the start, as he was playing against outstanding players from all over the state. Nick lost a few games initially while finding his feet, but then he started to fly.

I remember one tournament where he played the top player for his age group. I was standing right next to the boy's mother. She complained about her son having to play against a boy at a lower level and that it was a waste of their time. Karma is bittersweet as Nick thrashed this boy a year later.

✦

Tennis is expensive, especially when you reach the higher levels of the game. Grand Slam players win millions, but the cost of getting children to that level is staggering. Costs include coaching fees, tennis racket, restringing, tennis balls, travel, accommodation and tennis shoes.

I remember when Nick reached the tournament finals, and I went to get something from the car. The BMWs, Land Rovers, Mercedes, Lexus and other expensive cars in the car park made me feel like I was in another world. It showed that to get to that level of tennis, you had to be wealthy. We struggled financially with the costs associated with tennis, but somehow, we managed to get by.

In hindsight, I don't know how we did it, but as a parent, you will do anything to help your children achieve their dreams. As Nick worked his way up the tennis rankings, we were fortunate to have one of my mother's lovely and generous friends sponsor Nick. This took away much of the financial stress. He was also sponsored by *Head* for all his tennis rackets.

✦

Things were hard for James and Lily at the start. They would get dragged from one tennis tournament to another and miss out on hanging out with their friends. Eventually, they entered the tournaments themselves and enjoyed the trips away.

Chapter 9

The tennis incident

Nick climbed through the tennis rankings when he was eleven years old. Tennis coaches from all over were watching him as he had such a natural talent. I am saying this without my rose-coloured glasses.

However, one family, the *Smiths*, was unhappy with Nick's progress. The Smiths didn't like it when Nick beat their son, *Logan,* in a tournament. They were a funny family, as they would talk to us at some tournaments and not others. When they talked with us, the conversations weren't always about tennis. We talked about our careers and many other topics.

✦

It was a Saturday morning, and Nick played in a local round-robin tennis tournament. They played the best out of eight games rather than the typical three sets. Nick played the first game against Logan and beat him 8-0. That didn't go down well with Logan and his parents. Logan then played another boy straight away while Nick and his friends sat in the grandstand, watching.

Again, Logan was beaten 8-0. The boy who beat Logan followed protocol and put his hand out to shake his hand. Instead of shaking hands, Logan hit the net with his racket and stormed off the court. The boy who won stood there with his hand out as a harmless joke. Nick and his friends thought it was funny and started laughing. In no way were they laughing at Logan, but at the boy, who was still on the court with his hand out.

Now, picture in your mind the grumpiest, bitter woman you have ever seen in your life and replace her face with a Pitbull. This was Smith's mother. She stormed up to Nick and put her face right up to his, screaming, swearing, and even spitting on him. Amy got up to defend Nick, and she attacked her as well. The tournament organisers had to break things up. However, they didn't act against the behaviour as they were close family friends.

I had been working the morning shift at the hospital and arrived at the tennis courts just after the incident. I had parked my car when my daughter, Lily, came running up to tell me what happened, and she seemed distraught.

As I walked to the grandstand to learn more about what had happened, I saw the father, Bruce, sitting on the footpath. He stopped me and said that something had happened, and people would say things about his wife that weren't true. He seemed shaky and nervous while he was talking to me. I told him I would speak to my wife and decide for myself. The incident upset Amy and my kids, and everyone in the grandstand called the mother crazy.

We went home that afternoon, confused about how a family could let jealousy and envy overwhelm them with such anger. But that was just the start of what was to be over three years of torment towards my kids, myself, and Amy.

✦

The first attack from the Smiths was mind-blowing, and I don't mean that in a good way. It contributed to one of the many attempts on my life and the downfall of my nursing career. I was three-quarters of the way through my diploma in nursing and was working as a nursing assistant when I wasn't attending TAFE.

On the Wednesday following the weekend of the tennis tournament incident with the Smiths, I had just finished my shift at the hospital. I was going out the door when the hospital's CEO called me into his office. I sat at his meeting table, and he placed a manila envelope in front of me. I thought something great was about to happen. I had been working my ass off and getting great compliments from my nurse unit manager and my patients.

Maybe I was getting a pay rise?

I opened the envelope, which contained a typed letter. As I read it, I thought I was reading about somebody else. It was written as though it had come from a patient. This person stated that during their stay in the hospital, a nurse with a Kiwi accent inappropriately touched and fondled them. They also said that it happened every time no other nurses were around. The person did not sign the letter.

My initial thought was that the CEO would ask me if I knew of the person who may have done this. But then he said that only one other person in the hospital had a Kiwi accent and that they worked in a different ward. When I heard this, my eyes welled up with tears, and I wanted to climb under the table and curl into a ball. In a shaky, tearful voice, I responded that I would never do anything like that in a million years, nor would it cross my mind. I am not that type of person.

The CEO touched my shoulder and said he knew I would never do anything. However, due to company protocol, they would still have to investigate. He also said that the person would have put a name to the letter and taken legal action if the incident had happened. I cried all the way home and for the rest of the day and night. I wanted to end my life right there and then.

How could I continue living with people thinking I was that sort of person?

It put me into a deep depression.

When my mind was a little clearer the following day, I thought about things in more detail. I could remember the dates on the letter and that I wasn't working during those dates. I was at TAFE doing assessments and exams. I remembered a conversation with Bruce a few weeks earlier, telling him about my job and how hard it was to juggle TAFE and work. I told him about the ward I worked on, what type of work I did, and what my day comprised. I also told him the dates I was working, so he knew which tournaments Nick would be playing in. The dates I told Bruce I would work on had changed. It was then that I knew Bruce and his wife were responsible, but I had no way of proving it. It was their word against mine.

Following that letter, I felt like someone was constantly watching me. The hospital reduced my shifts and eventually transferred me to another ward, claiming they had enough shifts for me. I was devastated, as I had been doing well in my position and got on well with the other nurses. Amy had two similar letters sent to her work as well. Surely, someone wouldn't be trying to ruin our lives over a game of tennis.

A few months went by, and things had settled down a bit. We hadn't heard from or seen the Smiths at any tennis matches. Without knowing what was coming, it was the calm before the storm.

✦

The next incident happened at my child's primary school. Nick left early one morning to catch the bus to high school. He walked past his sibling's primary school to the bus stop. When he did, he saw what appeared to be a whole ream of A4 paper spread all over the road. He took little notice of it, as it could have been rubbish scattered from a bin or some pamphlets gone astray.

When my younger children went to school that morning, they found several teachers picking up hundreds of pieces of A4 paper from the road. My kids picked up one piece of paper. It had big photos of *Miss Piggy* on both sides and huge writing saying that they are pigs, cheats and that they have bipolar. My kids were so upset. The teachers sat with my kids for a while to help them through such a traumatic event and then sent them home for the day. I was furious, as I knew who was behind this. Who else would call us cheats, but the Smith family.

We took the paper to the police and told them who we thought was behind it. They couldn't do anything as there was no evidence, but they kept it on file in case it happened again. Things went quiet for a few months, and when we thought it had stopped, it raised its ugly head again.

It was a Saturday morning, and Nick was going to play a competition around the corner from his tennis club. When he arrived, he noticed thousands of paper strips on the tennis courts and the nearby playground. The paper strips had his name on one side and nasty messages about him on the other side. The tennis court owner was there, and she helped him pick them up. He was devastated and upset.

When was this going to end?

I was angry beyond words. I was now ninety-nine per cent sure who was doing this.

I took the paper strips to the police, and again, they wouldn't do anything as there wasn't enough evidence. All they did was file them with my previous paper drop complaint.

By this stage, I had been in and out of the hospital because of suicide attempts. This malicious attack on my son was not only taking a toll on my mental health but was bringing him down as well. I felt like a useless father, as I failed to protect my son from a psychopath three to four times his age. I couldn't even go to this guy's house and confront him, as he would deny everything. I didn't have enough proof that it was him. It would be his word against mine.

There was a gap of around three months before the next attack. This time, it was out in front of Nick's high school. A couple of Nick's friends approached him when he arrived at school and showed him some sheets of A4 paper scattered along the street. The papers showed a photo of me on one side and terrible words about Nick on the other. The side with me was from the newspaper when I was a missing person with a mental illness. Again, there were around five hundred sheets of paper. I was furious, embarrassed, and suicidal all rolled into one. If it weren't for wanting to be there for Nick, I would have ended my life right there and then.

Nick's mental health went downhill following this attack, as did James's and Lily's mental health. Nick wouldn't go to school until Amy or I had gone down and checked for any papers out front of the school. We did this very early every morning for quite some time. Some of Nick's friends from school would tease him about it. When I would pick him up from school, his friends would say, *hey Nick, the missing man is here to get you.*

Again, we took the sheets of paper to the police. This time, the police called Bruce and asked him to come to the station. He denied it, of course, but something he said confirmed my suspicions. He told the police that our family doesn't get on with anybody in the tennis community. This is when I realised it was him. We got on with everyone, and there wasn't one family that we didn't get on with.

✦

Now that I was confident that I knew the person who was behind these attacks on my family and myself, my blood was boiling. I am one of the most placid people you could ever meet. I trained and taught martial arts for years, and my instructors always taught me to walk away from fights and violence. But as these attacks had caused so much pain to me and my kids, I sat in my car outside the Smith's house at least twice a week. I would try to talk myself out of beating the shit out of him and subsequently putting myself in jail. He was an overweight, weak man who would attack you from a distance because he was too scared to approach you.

Six months to a year went by, and it started again right at the entrance to Nick's high school. Someone wrote the same missing person information on one side and nasty things about Nick on the other. This time, it was happening two to three times a week. Again, I had to go to the school early in the morning to check for paper drops and pick them up before the students arrived. There were even several nights when I sat in a tree on the school property waiting for him so I could try to catch him.

The malicious paper drops went on for quite some time. It was around three and a half years from the initial incident at the tennis courts. We thought it would never end until we met a lovely police officer who investigated further. She said this had gone on too long, and she could see how it was destroying our family. She couldn't believe that nothing had been done sooner. She coordinated with the high school and had a video camera installed to face the street outside the main entrance.

A few weeks went by, and nothing happened. I was worried Bruce had seen the camera and stopped, which would mean he had got away with over three years of tormenting our family. Then we hit the jackpot. At three in the morning, Bruce was caught on camera driving past the school. He threw a ream of printed A4 paper on the roof of his car. He then moved back and forth to spread the paper up and down the street.

Bruce was arrested and taken to the police station for questioning. Again, he denied everything, but that was until he was shown the video. Finally, he admitted to everything. It was lucky for us as they didn't have a shot of the number plate or a sharp image of Bruce driving the vehicle. They only had the model and colour of the car, which matched his.

Because Bruce was what the police called clean skin, meaning no prior convictions, he was let off easy. He received a two-year good behaviour bond, an apprehended violence order so that he couldn't go near my kids, and a fine. I was gutted as he nearly destroyed our lives. My kids needed counselling, and it affected my mental health severely. I felt like I had let my kids down as they had to endure this mental torture for so long.

So often, I wanted to take things into my own hands, as the police didn't take it seriously enough until the damage had been done. I don't have a violent bone in my body. Because of the severity of what was going on and how it was affecting my kids, some violent thoughts arose. I knew, though, that if I had dealt with the situation myself, I would have ended up in jail. That was where he needed to be, not me.

Chapter 10

Hospital, my second home

After my first stay in the private hospital, I tried my hardest to return to my everyday life. I attended TAFE, studied, worked, and spent the rest of my time with my beautiful children. Tennis had become our life, and we spent most weekends travelling to tennis tournaments. If we weren't at a tournament, we were hitting a ball at our local tennis courts.

My nursing diploma was progressing well. Initially, the assessments were difficult, as I hadn't studied since finishing my sign-writer apprenticeship. However, I got good marks and passed everything.

While doing my diploma, I worked as an assistant in nursing at our local private hospital. I was based in the surgical ward and cared for patients who had recently undergone surgery.

I enjoyed working in that ward; the other nurses treated me well, and I felt like part of a team. Things were going well, and I finally found something I enjoyed.

Unfortunately, when I thought life had changed for the better, the depression would raise its ugly head again. I succumbed to the pressure of trying to juggle work, study and tennis at the same time.

My mental health had declined. The dread of getting up in the morning and the thoughts of not wanting to be alive were constant. Everything became an effort, and even simple things like showering or getting out of bed became difficult. Then, the darkness hit me hard. I had to get out of this world. I was sick of living constantly with the pain in my head, the depression, the anxiety and the feeling that I was never good enough.

✦

One afternoon, Amy and I argued about what I wasn't doing around the house and my lack of motivation. It wasn't a serious argument, but more like a constructive conversation. I knew I wasn't contributing at home but didn't know how to pull myself out. The conversation was enough to tip me over the edge, and I cracked. I grabbed some medication from the cupboard and ran. I had no idea where I was going and no plans for what to do. I had to get away.

I had decided I was going to live on the street and become homeless. I would no longer have to worry about the financial stress and the pain I was putting my family through with my mental health challenges. All I would have to worry about was finding food and water for myself.

I didn't know about the services available to homeless people in my area. All I knew was that a lot of homeless people lived in Sydney, so I decided it would be a good place for me to go. The problem was that I had no money to get there, so I was stuck.

✦

I wandered around the streets and beaches aimlessly, feeling lost, hopeless, and extremely depressed. I had a minimal amount of medication with me, but took all of them in one go, hoping I would die. I knew they wouldn't do much, but I took them anyway. The only effect they had was to make me drowsy.

Sleeping in the open is rough when you don't have a blanket to keep you warm or a soft pillow to lay your head on. I would walk around for hours, searching for a place sheltered from the elements. I tried entrances to buildings and playgrounds and eventually found a beach hut to sleep in. It was cold and uncomfortable.

Food would be the next problem, as I had no money. I discovered the best place to find food was in a rubbish bin outside a fast-food restaurant. People would often throw half-eaten food away, but it tasted pretty good if you got to it fast enough.

✦

The thought of being found was frightening, and I decided that this was the life I wanted to live. I constantly looked around to ensure that no one I knew saw me. When the police would drive past, I would hide behind a tree.

Little did I know, I was on the local news as a missing person with mental illness. I was not only on the news, but also in the newspapers, radio, social media and the Internet. Years later, when someone did an Internet search, it would still come up with a photo and article about me as a missing person. At the very least, they could have chosen a better photo. They used the ugliest photo of me they could find.

✦

While on the street, I had time to think about my children and how much I missed them. I thought about the trauma they must be going through from having a dad who is missing. I don't know how long I was on the street, but I eventually realised that I was sick and in serious need of help. I can't remember what happened after that.

Did I take myself to the hospital, get found by the police, or go home?

Whatever happened, I was admitted to my local mental health private hospital.

I knew I was in for a lengthy stay in the hospital. Having spent three weeks there, I knew what to expect and was nowhere near as anxious as I had been during my previous stay.

✦

During this admission, I spent time in the courtyard smoking and getting to know other patients. I was lucky at the time to have received a large payment for selling prints of my art in Canada. This allowed me to buy cigarettes, as I was smoking at least a packet a day during my stay.

The hospital felt more like a nightclub than a mental health rehabilitation unit. This was because we would be in the courtyard partying until all hours of the morning, obviously without the alcohol. They cracked down on that and required patients to be in bed by a specific time. I think they also created a small smoking area so that people wouldn't smoke as much or offend people who weren't smokers.

It was quite a social place, and many intimate relationships were formed, which wasn't a good practice as it would lead to many issues. There were beanbags out in the courtyard, and they were so comfortable. They didn't last long, as some patients would hook up and have sex on them in the early morning hours. Little did they know cameras were everywhere around the hospital and the courtyard. The beanbags were eventually taken away.

Some afternoons, Amy and the kids would pick me up from the hospital, and we would go to the beach for a late lunch or dinner. Occasionally, Amy would bring the kids into the hospital to see me. Even though I had other patients to talk to, the hospital was a lonely place to be. I felt trapped and isolated from the rest of the world.

✦

There is one thing I learned through my mental health journey. You will not get the diagnosis, medication and therapy you need without sharing all the details about your past and present. The psychiatrist can only diagnose based on what you have shared with them.

I only shared the details of my marriage and current problems with my psychiatrist. I didn't share the rape, bullying, abandonment, highs and lows, and other traumas I had experienced. Because of this, I was diagnosed with situational depression, a diagnosis far from the correct one I later received.

A big part of why I ended up in the hospital, besides a major depressive episode, was financial pressures and the pressure to find additional employment. This caused many arguments between Amy and me when she came to visit me in the hospital.

On one of Amy's visits, we argued about our finances and the trauma that I was putting my kids through with my mental health. This triggered another bipolar depressive episode combined with extreme anger. When Amy left, I threw my phone across the room and then jumped on it, trying to smash it. Then I burst into tears and went back into the darkness of wanting to take my life.

It was during my meetings with my psychiatrist that we decided it would be better for my mental health to end my marriage to Amy. With me not handling and avoiding confrontation and the state I was in with my mental health, I got my psychiatrist to talk with Amy. This didn't go down well.

I couldn't handle the pain and guilt of breaking my family apart. I stormed out of the hospital and took an overdose of over-the-counter medication. The medication made me severely sick and drowsy, to the point where I was struggling to get off the ground. I decided I wanted help and that I wasn't ready to die, so I staggered back to the private hospital, where an ambulance was called. From there, they took me to the public hospital's emergency department.

I spent a week in the Psychiatric Emergency Care Centre (PECC) unit before they deemed me well enough to return to the private hospital. I was pretty fragile with my mental health while I was there. One day, I would bounce around with joy, and the next day, I would have severe depression where I could not function.

✦

Things were already strained between Amy and me. Amy also had a friend who was an inpatient who would add to the strain. She was intrusive, a troublemaker, and tried to ruin people's lives. She had *bitch* written all over her face.

One day, I was in the lift with a friend I had made in the hospital. She was an attractive blonde girl. We were laughing out loud and clowning around when the lift door opened, and Amy's friend was standing right in front of us. She just stood there, glaring and saying nothing. She told Amy I was having a relationship with someone in the hospital. This caused much anger and more damage to our already struggling marriage. It led to another suicide attempt and another stay in the PECC unit. It became a regular occurrence, and I had no control. I was eating and sleeping well, attending art classes, the gym (with a personal trainer) and therapy classes. But I didn't want to be alive.

I kept in close contact with my mum while in the hospital. Both Mum and I knew I was suffering from something much worse than situational depression. With our lack of knowledge about mental health, we could only rely on the psychiatrists' diagnosis.

I ended up spending three months in the private hospital with regular visits to the PECC unit at the public hospital. This would have cost the health insurance provider a small fortune, with hospital fees averaging around $1,000 a night.

Towards the end of my hospital stay, I was going to have to find another place to live as I had ended my marriage. I had made several friends in the hospital, including Jane, who owned a large house. I talked to her about my situation, and she was kind enough to offer me a place to stay. It was a huge relief, as I had nowhere to go. The thought of being homeless again was daunting.

The hospital released Jane and me on the same day, which worked well. Jane had a beautiful place. It was two stories with all the *mod cons*, including a large, stunning kitchen, three bathrooms, and plenty of bedrooms. She had a son in his twenties living with her, which would be very awkward for me. The main reason was that not long after moving into the house, Jane and I went from being flatmates to being in a relationship. Her son wasn't happy, and neither were my kids. Jane's son would call me *old mate*, as he didn't like me. I learned with my kids that it doesn't matter how long you have been separated from your partner; your kids never really accept you being in a new relationship. This can go on for years or indefinitely. Kids want their parents to be together and part of the family they grew up with.

Jane had a beautiful entertainment area at the back of her house. We would spend nearly every minute of the day and night sitting on the porch, smoking and drinking. We smoked so much that my mouth constantly felt like an ashtray. I would light a new cigarette from the one I was currently smoking before it went out. Our drinking was also out of control. Most nights of the week, we would keep drinking until we would almost pass out. I had never been a big drinker and am sure that the drinking contributed to another decline in my mental health.

I didn't realise at the time that one reason Jane had been in the hospital was because of alcohol dependence. The constant drinking together obviously didn't help with her addiction and exacerbated it. She was caught at one stage taking a bottle of expensive spirit from her son's room. He ended up having to put a lock on his door. I felt guilty when I found out the main reason she was in the hospital, as I would have contributed to her addiction.

One thing I enjoyed while living with Jane was her delicious meals. She was a great cook, and I never went hungry. She was very proud of her cooking abilities.

My kids were angry when I started the relationship with Jane, as they thought it had begun in the hospital. They hated Jane passionately and didn't enjoy coming to see me at her house. They desperately wanted me to be back with their mum. It was a challenging position for me as they wouldn't talk to Jane, and I felt like I was always trying to keep the peace. I tried to explain to them how important Jane was to me and asked them if they could try to get on with her. Things became quite strained with my kids, which was not good for my mental health. I love my kids to bits, and they are the most important people in my life. I understood how they felt and was guilty of what I was putting them through.

✦

While living with Jane, I became interested in photography. I loved taking photos of people, especially nudes. I am not a perverted person, and that wasn't the reason that I loved nude photography. I loved the body form and how the camera captured the body's beautiful lines, curves, shadows and highlights. I especially loved black-and-white photography.

To improve my photography skills, I joined a photography group, where I could develop my passion for the craft. The person who ran the group was a well-established French photographer. She had made a name for herself in boudoir and nude photography.

Photographers would pay two hundred dollars to attend her mansion at a popular beach resort to take photos of naked women. The models would do a variety of different poses over four hours. It was a great opportunity to learn new skills, especially from the other photographers.

The photography sessions were not always at her mansion. We would go to beaches and various other locations. One photo shoot comprised a three-day trip to some old ruins. There were twelve photographers and two models who attended the photo shoot.

We formed two groups of six and had a model for each group. We then swapped models halfway through the day. The models would start in boudoir clothing and spend the rest of the day naked. The photos were amazing, and I got a small prize for being the best photographer. Of course, I thought it was a fluke that my photos were so good. The imposter syndrome was talking again.

We stayed in some old farmhouses half an hour's walk from the ruins. It was a beautiful area surrounded by trees and mountains. We all got a room each, which was a relief, as I don't like sharing a room with anyone. I will never forget my first night, though. I woke up in the middle of the night with something tickling my face.

Whatever it was, I brushed it off my face and tried to go back to sleep. After it happened a few times, I thought I had better get up to check what it was. I wish I hadn't. Sitting on the floor beside the bed was a large blue spider, bigger than a huntsman, one of Australia's biggest spiders.

Now, I have a phobia of spiders. There was no way I would stay in that bedroom, so I went and slept on the lounge in the living room.

Well, wasn't that a mistake.

I rolled over onto my back and looked up at the ceiling. Above me were about ten huntsman spiders the size of my hand.

This is crazy!

I grabbed my stuff and was straight out the front door. I slept in my car for the next two nights.

✦

One symptom of living with bipolar is the need to spend excessive amounts of money, especially when you are experiencing mania or hypomania.

When I experienced hypomania, I would overspend and put myself in financial hardship. Most of the money I spent was on photography equipment, as I had decided to be the best photographer in the world. I was going to be world-renowned for my amazing nude photography.

I don't know how, but I got a loan from the bank for $30,000. I used the money to buy the most expensive camera and bought several lenses worth more than the camera itself. I bought studio lighting and backdrops to set up my photography studio. I never gave a thought about how I was going to pay any of this money back. When I bought all the photography equipment, I also bought a car to get to my photo shoots. So, I went to the local car dealer in my area and bought a brand-new car for $30,000.

Now, how the hell was I going to pay that off?

✦

Paul Anthony

I was on a quest to be the best nude photographer in the world. I never thought about how Jane felt about me taking photos of naked women. To me, it was art, but everyone has a different perception of nudity.

When I think back now, I had organised one private photo shoot, which would have been quite concerning and confronting for Jane. I sat her down several times and explained to her that my photography was art and nothing sexual. I never looked at my models sexually, which many people couldn't understand. After attending the photography group several times, I decided I would have a go at setting up my own photo shoot. After researching online, I made several phone calls and found a model willing to pose for me. She was a well-established model and married, so I felt safe booking her for the shoot.

I organised a photo shoot in a hotel room an hour and a half from where I lived with Jane. The room was beautiful. It had a well-lit lounge area with a mezzanine floor, which allowed me to take photos above the model.

Jane asked me to drop her off at a local pub on the way up to the photoshoot. She wanted to catch up with some girlfriends for a few drinks, and I would pick her up on the way home.

The model was pleasant to work with. We started off shooting lingerie and then moved to full nudes. She felt comfortable around me and was in a safe space. The photoshoot was a success, and I got lots of great photos. Afterwards, I packed up all my gear, said goodbye to the model, and returned home. On the way, I stopped at the pub to pick up Jane.

When I walked into the pub, I couldn't find Jane anywhere as the pub was busy. After ten minutes of searching, I found some of her friends. They told me Jane was not doing well and pointed me towards her. Jane was leaning against the bar, swaying all over the place. I could see that she was very drunk.

Just before I got to her, she fell on the floor. She was a mess. I picked her up, leaned her against the bar, and asked her what she was doing. She said she had lost her mobile phone, and the bartender refused to serve her a drink. The phone was behind the bar with the bartender, who held onto it until security arrived.

Now I had to get Jane out of the pub and into the car. I got under her arm and assisted her, which took some time. There were many falls, and we went backward and forward. Everyone we walked past laughed at us and must have looked funny.

When we got home, I had to get her into the house. This was much harder than getting her out of the pub, as we had thirty steps to tackle before we got to the front door. I don't know if her excessive drinking was related to the nude photoshoot or if it was alcohol dependence. I think it was a combination of both. Things got quite strained between Jane and me after that incident, and the drinking and smoking became more regular.

Jane and I were invited to a party at one of her family friends' houses one day. They lived right on the bank of a beautiful river. Quite a few families and friends turned up. This was not good for me, as I am uncomfortable around a lot of people. This is because I have extreme social anxiety and need to leave in a hurry.

Jane and I had set up a tent next to the river and walked over to where all the people were partying. After a short time, I got anxious, so I told Jane that I wasn't feeling well and needed to return to the tent. I climbed into the tent, zipped it up, and curled into a fetal position on the mattress. I was shaking with anxiety, and things got worse after I lay down. I experienced extreme suicidal thoughts. I wanted to take my life.

Where the hell did this come from?

I had thoughts of jumping into the river and drowning myself. The thoughts got stronger and stronger, to the point that I needed to call someone. I got the courage to call one of the suicide prevention services. The lady who answered the phone seemed harsh and not empathetic to what I was going through. I could also tell from her questions that she would call the police and an ambulance.

I started to backtrack and say I was feeling better and would be okay. I didn't want the police or an ambulance to come out. I was staying on somebody else's property; how embarrassing would that be? Eventually, after lying my ass off, the lady agreed I was doing better. She said someone would call me the next day to check in, and I ended the call.

I wasn't feeling any better, so I lay down in a fetal position for a few hours before I could get to sleep. Jane arrived back at some crazy morning hour and woke me up. I wasn't in a state where I could talk, even though I probably wouldn't have.

When I woke up the following day, I still wasn't feeling well and was still thinking I would be better off dead. I told Jane that I had called a suicide prevention service and that I was doing okay, even though I was only surviving. I put my fake happy face on and continued for the rest of the day before we returned home.

✦

My mental health kept going downhill, and I struggled to control it. It was most likely a combination of the distance that was forming between my kids and me, and Jane's constant drinking. Oh, and don't forget my undiagnosed bipolar. One morning, I decided I was going to take some medication that I was prescribed to help me sleep. I was suffering badly from insomnia and was having nightmares. Instead of taking one pill, I took three and ended up sleeping from that morning to the following afternoon. I was so confused when I awoke, as I had slept for two days.

How the hell did I sleep for that long? How had I gone that long without going to the toilet?

✦

While working on the medical ward of the hospital, I was nearing the end of my diploma. I enjoyed working as an assistant in nursing and looked forward to becoming a qualified enrolled nurse and pursuing my dream of working in a theatre. But things were about to turn bad big time!

I had been asked to do some shifts on the medical ward at the hospital. I was looking after an older man who would constantly pull out his catheter, which caused an infection, and he was put on a drip. My job was to ensure he didn't pull his catheter out and change the saline bag before it ran out. I was to be looking after this man throughout my entire shift.

Halfway through the day, I received a call from the government-funded organisation sponsoring my diploma. Without them, I wouldn't have been able to get the diploma, as it would have cost me $15,000. There is no way that I would have been able to pay for that.

The person on the phone advised me that my application for the funding had been rejected.

Rejected?

I told them it had been approved fifteen months ago when I started the course. She said that an error had been made, and I didn't meet the requirements for the funding because I was not an Australian citizen. I said I had come to Australia in 1999 when visas weren't required. I am classed as having a special category visa and was a permanent resident.

I argued with them over the phone. This can't be real. I was told I must pay $15,000 to complete the course.

How the hell was I going to pay for that?

After spending ridiculous amounts of money on camera equipment and a car, there was no way I could get another loan for $15,000.

I had two more assignments to complete, and my diploma was finished. I would have been an endorsed enrolled nurse. I called local parliament members and everyone I thought could help me. TAFE advised they couldn't help me and denied being the one who had made the error. To add salt to the wound, I discovered that I would have been accepted for funding if I had gone through the university.

The following day, I was told I couldn't work as I was no longer insured by TAFE if something happened while working at the hospital. It didn't matter how much I argued or tried to find $15,000. There was nothing I could do.

Fifteen months of study, assignments and placements had gone down the drain. I could no longer finish my diploma and could not work as a nurse.

✦

My mental health spiralled out of control. I was angry, depressed and had so much hate towards the world. I wanted to die. *What was the point of living anymore?* My kids hated me. I was unemployed and had lost my chance of getting a nursing qualification. My life was over.

I plucked up the courage to call the sign company I worked for before entering nursing. The timing was perfect; one designer had just left, and I could fill his role. Unfortunately, this didn't improve how I felt about my life. I felt like I had taken a huge step backward by returning to my old job. I should have been thankful that I had a job at all. I was also offered much less money than when I initially worked for the company.

✦

Around the same time, I was going through all the issues with my now non-existent nursing career. Amy and her mum started the law proceedings to sort out the joint finances and the house.

I sensed that Amy's mum didn't like me much. At annual events such as birthdays, I felt like I didn't fit in, and nobody was interested in how my life was going. So, I spent most of the time with my kids, which I really loved.

The legal proceedings began, and I received papers regarding our house, car, and other financial matters. I had to get a lawyer. This was hard. I had left the family home with nothing, but the clothes on my back and no money. Thankfully, I found a lovely lawyer who would deduct her fees from my settlement money.

My lawyer communicated regularly with Amy's lawyer, hoping we would reach an agreement quickly. As with most legal negotiations, it went back and forth for a long time. Just when you thought it was sorted, another change would come through.

I was struggling with my mental health and couldn't keep going. It was killing me. The tension between Amy and me was horrible, and it felt like Amy and her mum were at war with me. On the next visit to my lawyer, I told her I couldn't do it anymore. I signed over everything and took a small amount to cover my lawyer's fees. I felt good about the decision, even though I would have to start life from scratch with nothing. It was comforting to know my kids would have a roof over their heads and wouldn't have to move away from their school and friends. I am sure Amy's anger towards me was due to my ending the marriage and quickly moving into another relationship, which is understandable. Relationships are hard to navigate at the best of times without throwing mental illness into the mix.

✦

My life was falling apart, and things between Jane and me rapidly declined. Jane went and stayed with her parents for a few days so we could have a break. By this stage, I had reached breaking point. To hell with this world. I was checking out. I entered Jane's bathroom and took a few packets of her over-the-counter medications out of her medicine cabinet.

I took as many pills as I could. At first, I felt sleepy, and then the nausea and vomiting started. To top things off, I was vomiting blood. The bathroom looked like a war zone. I was extremely weak, drowsy, and struggling to stand. I was also scared. This wasn't going as planned. I needed help, so I crawled to the phone in the lounge room and called the ambulance. They took me to the emergency department and administered charcoal to counteract the overdose. They admitted me to the PECC unit, where I spent the following week.

✦

When I left the PECC unit, I returned to Jane's house, but things weren't good between us. Nothing was mentioned about what happened. It was like the elephant in the room.

Jane was drinking more than usual, and we had more arguments. We needed to get away from each other, so I moved into one of her bedrooms downstairs. It was, without doubt, the worst thing I could have done. It made things between us a lot worse, especially when she was drunk.

My kids were feeling even more uncomfortable about coming around to see me, so I decided it was time to move out. I had no idea where I would go. I knew I needed to find somewhere else, hopefully, where I could rebuild my relationship with my kids.

Chapter 11

Instabilities

After a few weeks, I found a nice little unit near my kids' home. It was one of four units on a busy street, but it was my space, and I could come and go as I wanted. Amy was kind enough to give me furniture she didn't need for the house. My mum sent me money from New Zealand to help me source everything required to set up my unit. I was set, ready to go. Maybe this will be the change I need in my life.

While living in my unit, things were okay for the first few months, but I struggled to rebuild my relationship with my kids. They were still angry with me for living with Jane and upset and angry that their mum and I were not together.

I can only recall my kids staying with me once, despite having a spare room in my unit, which I had made available for them. I was very sad as I wanted to rebuild my bond with them and improve things. I couldn't understand why they were so angry at the time, but I know now.

✦

Some new neighbours moved in next door a few months after I moved into my unit. They were young, rough, had never rented, and had no respect for others. Their television would be up so loud that I couldn't even hear my own television. They would park their car in front of my bedroom window and constantly have loud parties all night. Sleep is an important thing for someone living with mental illness, and I wasn't getting any. I lost count of the times I would ask them to keep the noise down or to turn their television down.

One day, they played footy out in front of my unit and kept kicking the ball into my car and bedroom window. I tried talking to them politely about the issues, but it almost became a physical confrontation.

✦

After living in my unit for around five months, extreme bipolar depression raised its ugly head again. Everything that was going on around me added to the depression, and it spiralled out of control.

I couldn't hold a relationship. I felt like my kids hated me and I had the neighbours from hell. On top of this, I was lonely. I don't cope on my own and need people around me to survive. Loneliness makes me feel like I am suffocating; it is a cruel feeling.

Early one morning, I woke up, and it was still dark outside. I had a feeling in my body that is hard to describe. It was like a feeling of doom, like the world had ended, and I was the only one living there.

My head was racing and full of negative thoughts. I tried to go back to sleep, but it didn't happen, so I took double the amount of my antidepressant tablets. After that, I took a long, hot shower, but that didn't work. I tried everything, but I couldn't stop how I felt. I fought as hard as I could, but I lost the battle.

Should I call someone? Should I call an ambulance?

It was too late. My mind was telling me I was not worthy of life. I was wasting oxygen, and nobody wanted me in this world.

I had been battling the demons in my head all day. When the sun went down, I decided it was time to end the battle and take my life. The world would be a better place for it. I took all my medications out of my cupboard and took every single one. I can't remember much after taking the drugs other than waking up on a hospital bed with a drip in my arm.

Who called the ambulance? How did they get into my unit?

✦

Following this attempt on my life, I was put in the psychiatric ward for three weeks in the public hospital system. If you have never stayed in a public ward, you are lucky. They are the scariest places, but they keep you safe from harming yourself or others. For someone who has never been in a psychiatric ward, they can be confronting.

The ward is set up differently from a standard hospital ward. There is a long corridor with around ten small bedrooms on each side containing a hospital bed and a locked cupboard. There is a window in your room that is fully secured and can't be opened, and you can't see out of it. The door to your room has a small window facing the hallway, allowing nurses to check in on you.

Two or three rooms down the hallway contain shared showers and toilets. The nurse's station is at the front of the ward, which is closed with protective glass. The nurses only come out to give you meds when accompanied by another nurse for their safety. I don't know why they did this, as I found it a safe place to be.

Next to the nurse's station was a lounge room with one television. A larger room with tables, seating and a table tennis table connected to the lounge. Within this room is a large steel wall with holes through which you can see out, but can't see in. There was a small lunchroom that provided breakfast, lunch and dinner.

The standard length of stay in the psychiatric ward was three weeks, depending on the severity of your case. Some people were voluntary patients, but most were scheduled. This means you must stay in the hospital until deemed fit to leave following a review by the hospital psychiatrist.

There were several times when I tried to convince the psychiatrist that I was ready to leave before the three weeks were up. Thankfully, they knew better. I was always scheduled when I went to the hospital, and all my trips were via ambulance except for one.

I haven't painted a pretty picture of what a psychiatric ward is like. However, they are the safest place to be when you are in extreme distress and planning to take your life. I wouldn't be here if I hadn't been scheduled to stay there. It saved my life. I highly recommend attending the hospital if you are distressed and have suicidal thoughts.

Understanding mental health and suicide is slowly evolving. There are several services available or under development as an alternative to hospital treatment.

✦

Through my lived experience of suicidal behaviour, I have learned that there are two main types.

Someone living with mental illness may have suicidal thoughts associated with emotional or psychological pain and want this pain to stop. Suicidal thoughts are serious and a dark place to be, but they don't always lead to a suicide attempt.

A suicide attempt is when someone tries to take their life. A mental health specialist can prevent a suicide attempt, especially when someone seeks help while experiencing suicidal thoughts. Sadly, others will attempt to take their lives on the spur of the moment with no planning.

If someone plans an attempt, they won't seek help and may hide it from others. I planned most of the attempts to take my life without seeking help. If a specialist asked me if I had a plan, I would never tell them. They weren't going to stop what I desired. That was the worst thing I could have done if I wanted to save myself.

When I talk to people today, I stress how important it is to share how you are feeling, as suicide is preventable. There is hope, even though you don't see it.

✦

During the worst eight to ten years of my life, I had no desire to live. I hated life and was just existing. When I say that I hated life, I still loved my kids more than anything. I have had so many people ask me how I could do that to my kids. This comment is a prime example of how people don't understand what you are experiencing when you want to end your life. I wanted to escape the pain of living with mental illness. During this extreme state of mind, I didn't think I would hurt my kids through my actions. I thought they would be better off and happier without me.

Suicide had become my safety blanket. I didn't want to be alive, so if anything went wrong in my life, suicide would be my solution.

✦

Following my suicide attempt while living in the unit by myself, I decided it would be safer if I shared a house with someone else. I had to decide whether to move closer to work, an hour's drive away, or stay closer to my kids. I moved closer to work as things were tight financially, and I would save on travel costs. The kids were still upset with me, and I wouldn't usually see them until the weekend. It was easier to drive and see them on the weekend than to drive for an hour to get to work five days a week. I found shared accommodation near Amy's mother so that when the kids came to see their grandmother, they could also see me. It worked out to be a good decision.

The lady who owned the unit and became my flatmate was a beautiful soul, one of the loveliest people you could ever meet. There was no attraction between us, which made things more comfortable when sharing with the opposite sex. She treated me well and made me feel like it was my home. We became close friends while living there.

There were a couple of awkward moments for me during my stay there. My flatmate had a long-distance relationship with a guy. They would talk to each other most nights on the computer, but I don't think she realised how thin the walls were. More noises were coming from that room than I wanted to hear.

With my flatmate spending more and more nights in her room talking with her partner, I became quite lonely. As I didn't do well with loneliness, I became depressed again. Hence, I decided I would try looking for another relationship. I scrolled through the dating sites, and it wasn't long before I got a match. She was attractive, owned her own house, and seemed successful. Initially, I felt a little intimidated by her, as I thought I was too ugly. I was embarrassed that, at my age, I had nothing to show for all the years I had worked. My unit was nice, but my room was relatively small. The agreement with my flatmate was that I couldn't have anyone over to stay.

How is a grown man supposed to share that with his potential new partner? But I thought, what the hell? I will give this girl a go and see what happens. I mean, what is the worst thing that can happen?

After two weeks of texting and talking, we went on a dinner date. I booked dinner for us at a Returned Services League club within walking distance of where I was living.

Sometimes, people put younger, modified photos of themselves on dating sites, but she was way more attractive than her photo. It made me nervous as I had low self-esteem and low confidence. *What was she doing with me?* I am only an average, if not ugly, guy. I felt this would not go well. The date started okay; we had similar interests, and the conversation flowed without effort.

After a few drinks, she said she had to tell me something that might put me off her and make me run. To make her feel at ease, I said I was open-minded, and she could tell me anything. She told me she was into bondage and loved being tied up, whipped, and spanked with a paddle until she bled. Well, I just about fell off my seat. That was the last thing I expected her to say. She asked me what I thought about it. I was shocked and didn't know how to respond.

I thought that the best way to handle this was with honesty. I told her how I don't like hurting people, had never hit a woman, and had no intention of doing so. After she told me more about what was involved, which included leaving some nasty welts on the body, I said I would give it a go to take away the awkwardness of the moment. I quickly changed the topic of conversation, and the rest of the date went well.

I had to seriously consider whether I wanted to go on a second date.

Am I going to provide her with the pain that she was after?

We texted and talked on the phone for a couple of weeks. We agreed to meet again and go for a bush walk down the coast. The bush walk went well, although it was a little out there for a second date. She needed to go to the toilet, so she squatted right in front of me. I didn't know where to look.

On the way home in the car, she asked about something that I found extremely disturbing, which ended the possibility of the relationship progressing. She was attending an event in the city and asked if I would like to join her. There would be a large group of people who would get together to act out various fetishes.

Where the hell was this going?

She explained the women would dress like babies, wearing nothing, but a nappy and a dummy. She would behave exactly like a baby, as in cry, poo and wee. I would pretend to be her father and change her nappy after she had gone to the toilet. This was wrong in so many ways. I did not know what to say and was in shock.

Because I hated confrontation, I called her from work the next day and told her I didn't think we were suited to each other. Well, she got angry and started yelling at me on the phone. She said she had opened up to me as she thought she could trust me. I wish she didn't, as it haunted me for quite some time to believe that people would do such a thing.

✦

I was too scared to go on another dating site after that. It was too confronting and disturbing for me. I was traumatised.

How was I going to meet somebody now? Was I going to be single for the rest of my life?

After a few weeks, I thought I could hook up with someone I already knew. I met a few lovely girls while I was in the hospital. They would understand my mental health journey. I wouldn't have to hide it out of fear that they would leave me when they found out. Perfect solution.

I remembered a girl named Jade, with whom I often talked while I was in the hospital. We got on well, and I liked her, but she had a boyfriend. I looked her up on Facebook anyway, as maybe she was single now. Sure enough, when I looked her up, her relationship status showed as single. So, I sent her a friend request, and she accepted. We talked via Facebook Messenger for the next couple of weeks.

Jade and I would end up meeting at her place the following week. She lived with her son, who had autism. This was hard for me at the start. Having worked with people who live with autism, I knew how hard it must have been for them, and they were supportive and understanding.

I would later discover that his behavioural issues weren't related to autism. This made it hard for Jade and me to spend quality time together. Jade would drink regularly and in large quantities, which, when I look back now, I think was her way of coping. She was a great mum and loved her son to bits.

As I had experienced in previous relationships, I found I didn't cope well with someone who drank a lot. I would end up drinking a lot myself, which wasn't the best for my mental health. I put it down to having grandparents with alcohol dependence when I was a child.

Jade lived with diabetes and often had diabetic attacks. She had a permanent insulin pump to monitor her glucose levels. There was always lemonade and jellybeans on hand to bring her out of an attack when required.

One night, we went to the local footy club for dinner and some drinks. We found ourselves at a table and decided that I would order dinner while Jade went and got us a drink. Jade was at the table when I returned, but there were no drinks. I asked her why she hadn't got the drinks, and she mumbled the bartender had refused to serve her. Jade seemed wobbly and slurred her words. I figured she was recovering from a diabetic attack and suggested I go to the bar and get the drinks.

While at the bar, I asked the bartender why he had refused to serve Jade. He told me he isn't allowed to serve drinks to someone who is visibly drunk. I had a go at him, saying that Jade had diabetes and wasn't drunk. We had spent the day together before going to the club, and I hadn't seen her drinking.

The bartender told me she had previously been kicked out of the club for being drunk and violent. He said security had removed her several times, and the club banned her. I refused to believe what I was hearing. We had our meal and a few drinks and left. I thought the bartender was rude and mixed up Jade with someone else.

As the weeks passed, I noticed Jade slurring her words and sometimes becoming aggressive. I suspected something more was happening than I knew about, but I didn't know what. It couldn't be alcohol, as I had never seen her drink during the day.

✦

One day, Jade asked me if I wanted to go on a cruise as she had found an Internet site with large discounts. I told Jade I couldn't afford to go on a cruise because I had no money and was struggling with my debts. She said not to worry and that she would cover the upfront cost. She also said I could pay her back over time, and if I couldn't, that was also okay.

Before the trip, we decided I would move into Jade's place, as I had been spending a lot of time there. So, sadly, I gave my notice to my current flatmate and moved all my belongings into Jade's house.

The cruise came around fast, and I was quite excited. We were overwhelmed by the ship's massive size when we arrived at the port, where it was moored. The ship was even more impressive inside. There were several levels with bars, casinos, kids' clubs, theatres and fun activities. We had quite a large room with a balcony. This was going to be my dream holiday. The trip lasted four nights, and we spent most of our time doing kids' activities with Jade's son. We also sat around the pool drinking while Jade's son went swimming. Her son was the trip's focus, which didn't bother me, but he would throw a tantrum if he didn't get his way.

Jade drank excessively on the cruise. She would start when the bar opened and stop when it closed. As soon as she finished a drink, she would be at the bar getting another one. I had never seen anyone drink so much; I couldn't keep up. This caused problems with her diabetes, and we returned to the room several times. I had to get some sugar into her system and hold her legs in the air to settle her.

It got to the last night of the trip, and I had enough of her excessive drinking, so I addressed the issue. Well, that didn't work, and she got aggressive towards me, as she was drunk from drinking throughout the day. I thought giving her some space would be a good idea. So, I headed up to the smoking area at the top of the ship.

I had only been sitting in the smoking area for about half an hour when Jade stormed past me at speed. I tried to call her over, but she just glared at me and kept walking. All I could think about at the time was where her son was.

Has she left him in the room by himself? Was he okay?

I headed back to our room and checked on him. Thankfully, he was asleep in bed.

How could she leave him by himself?

I thought about looking for Jade, but decided to wait for her in the room if her son woke.

After a couple of hours, Jade still hadn't returned. Her son was still asleep, but I knew he would freak out if he woke up and his mum wasn't there. So, I decided I had to look for her. I went to different locations around the ship and returned every ten minutes to check if her son was okay.

It was extremely late, and everything on the ship was closed. I was getting worried. Then I remembered a nightclub at the other end of the ship. I knew this was a place Jade could keep drinking into the night, so I headed there to look.

I finally found her, but I was dumbfounded by what I saw. She was on the dance floor, being intimate and passionately kissing another guy. That was the last straw, but I was still worried about her son and had to get her back to her room. I went to the dance floor and approached Jade. I said she should return to the room as her son might wake up and freak out. Her response was *piss off; I can do what I want.* The guy she was with also told me to get lost and pushed me away.

I was concerned at this stage, so I approached two security guards who were already watching Jade because of her being so drunk. I explained the situation, and they offered to help me get her back to the room. She argued with the security guards and reluctantly went with them. Jade was all over the place on the way back to the room. She was constantly bumping into walls and falling over. Eventually, we returned to the room, and things got violent. The security guards entered the room to calm Jade and ensure she was okay. However, she became more aggressive and attacked them.

During the screaming match with the guards, she said I physically abused her earlier in the night and didn't want me back in the room.

Shit, are you kidding me?

I didn't have an abusive bone in my body. The security guards suggested it would be a good idea if I accompanied them to the bottom of the ship and stayed there for the night.

I don't think they knew who to believe. I sat in a chair at the bottom of the ship for the rest of the night and got no sleep. In the early morning hours, I told the security guards what had happened. They were so apologetic that they kept me at the bottom of the ship for the night. They said that Jade would be banned from going on a cruise on any of their ships, but I would be okay.

The morning came around, and it was time to depart the ship. I got off as quickly as possible, as I didn't want to see Jade again. Then I realised that there was a problem. All my belongings were at Jade's house, and I had nowhere to go. I would at least have to return to the house to get my stuff.

I was one of the first off the ship as I left early. I hoped I had enough time to return to the house before Jade and get my belongings. By the time I got back to the house, Jade was already there, as she had got a lift from her father. I had no idea how I would be greeted when I opened the door. To my surprise, she was very apologetic. She wrapped her arms around me and said she felt terrible for what she had done. I was stupid, accepted the apology, and gave things another go. I should have run.

✦

As time went on, I learned some things about Jade that were quite concerning. She told me she had a criminal record and that she had bitten a chunk out of a security guard's arm. She denied she was in the wrong and said that he had hit her first. Yeah right.

The slurring of her words and issues with her diabetes were getting considerably worse. I became increasingly suspicious that there was more going on than met the eye. Maybe the bartender at the club was right, and she had been banned from the club for being a violent drunk. I had to investigate for myself. Maybe she was drinking more than I knew, and she was hiding alcohol somewhere in the house.

One day, I waited for Jade to go to the supermarket to get some food and searched the entire house for alcohol. I looked in all the cupboards and every place where you could hide alcohol. I couldn't find anything. Then I remembered some people hide things under their mattresses. Sure enough, when I lifted the mattress, there were many empty bottles of vodka. I noticed she would often go to the toilet, which was connected to her bedroom, and she would be gone for quite some time. She was sneaking into her room and drinking large amounts of straight vodka. Maybe the glasses of lemonade she drank to help with her diabetes were full of vodka, too.

After contemplating what to do, I confronted her about what I had found. Well, did she get upset. How dare I go through her house and suggest she had a drinking problem. She became very aggressive. I have never been yelled at like that before. It was like she was possessed. It took a few days before she calmed down, but she still denied she had a problem.

✦

A couple of days after finding the alcohol, I had my kids come over to stay for the night. They hadn't stayed over before, as they didn't like Jade much at all. I noticed Jade had been hitting the alcohol quite hard that morning and was drunk. I took the kids out for the day and returned to the house when it was time for bed. The next day, Jade was unhappy that we were going to go out again without her and her son. So, I changed my plans and stayed home to keep the peace.

My kids couldn't do anything right that day. Jade would get angry and yell at them over nothing. By the end of the day, my kids were sitting in a chair, too scared to move. It got worse by the minute, so I confronted her about how she treated my kids. We left the house to talk, and *World War Three* broke out. She turned into a psychopath. I had never seen anything like it before.

After ten minutes of Jade going ballistic, I decided it was time to leave. I didn't worry about getting any of my stuff and just had to get my kids out of there. She followed us to the car and up the driveway, yelling her head off. As I drove away, Jade sent me abusive texts, one after the other. My phone kept pinging constantly. It was awful.

Chapter 12

Beginning of the end

I cried most of the way to my kids' house. *What had I done to them?* I had put my kids in danger and had traumatised them. They were so upset. I dropped my kids off at home and felt sick to my stomach. *What do I do now? How can I live with myself after what I have done to my kids?* I had nowhere to live now, as I couldn't go back to Jade's house.

My thoughts instantly turned to suicide, as they always did when things got bad. I didn't deserve to be alive, and I believed my kids, and everyone would be better off without me. I had done so much damage to my kids with the last two relationships. I'm such a shit father. I sat in my car at the end of the street and contemplated what I would do next. I decided there and then that I was going to take my life.

How could I do it with no pain and would go peacefully?

I had decided what I was going to do. I was going to drive to a remote location and gas myself. My first stop was the hardware store to get what I needed to complete the job. Now, I had to decide where to do it so I wouldn't get caught.

I must have driven around for hours looking for a place where I could park my car in a place where nobody could find me. Finally, I found a spot hidden by trees, away from houses. Nobody could find me there. I hooked everything up to my car, started the car and lay back in my seat, waiting to die.

Hang on a minute. I hadn't told my kids I loved them, so I called Amy and asked her to tell them I loved them. She asked me why, and I told her I was leaving the world and making it a better place for everyone. Amy tried to find out where I was, but I wouldn't tell her. In my half-conscious state, I vaguely recall telling her the suburb I was in so they knew where to look for my body. I turned my phone off, fell asleep, and was finally at peace, or so I thought.

✦

I don't know how long I had been unconscious, but I vaguely remember being pulled out of my car onto the ground. Everything was hazy, and I was in and out of consciousness. The last thing I remember is seeing an ambulance and police cars.

I woke up in the hospital, very sick, and was connected to a drip. They tested me to see how much carbon dioxide I had in my body. The treating psychiatrist attended my bedside and told me how lucky I was. *Lucky*, I thought, *I am still bloody alive. How is that lucky?* Eventually, I was moved to the psychiatric ward, which was a place that I hated. I would learn later that it was the safest place for me. I was so angry and still wanted out. I wanted to die.

I was put in a room farthest away from the nurse's station and left alone to sit in my misery and anger. I curled up in a fetal position on the bed. My head was still in a very dark place. While in my room, I noticed the nurses would come around and check on me every half an hour. I started looking around for something to finish the job. I came up with a plan to hang myself. It was going to work; I had found a solution.

I waited for the nurses to do their rounds and followed my plan, but one nurse returned to check on me earlier than expected. They hit the alarm, and all the staff came running. I was so angry and pissed off.

Why did everyone have to stop me? It is my life! Let me go.

I ended up being moved to a room opposite the nurse's station. They took my sheets, blankets, towels, clothes and anything that I could use to take my life. I felt humiliated, and they were treating me like an animal, but they were only trying to save my life.

They released me to other parts of the ward the following day. There were a lot of people around, but I kept to myself. I didn't want to speak to anyone. I was super depressed, the worst I had ever felt in my life. It took a week before my suicidal thoughts were reduced.

Amy would bring the kids to see me, and we would meet in a room outside the ward. Sometimes, I thought of running, but luckily, they would lock me in the room. I couldn't look my kids in the eyes, and when I did, I would see the pain that I was putting them through. I can't imagine how hard it must have been for them to have a father who kept trying to take his life.

Why did their father want to leave them?

I thought they would be better off without me.

I ended up seeing the psychiatrist two times while I was in the ward. Once was to find out about me and talk about a diagnosis. The other time was to check to see if I was fit to leave the hospital at the end of my three-week stay. As per every visit to the hospital, I was scheduled and couldn't leave unless the psychiatrist thought I was safe to do so. The psychiatrist diagnosed me with borderline personality disorder. I would find out later that the diagnosis was wrong. Wrong diagnoses would contribute to some of the darkest times in my life.

During a visit with Amy and the kids, Amy asked if I would like to stay in the rumpus room under her house. I was so relieved and thankful, as I had nowhere to go.

Things would not be the same moving back in with Amy. After all, we had been separated for nearly two years. I had been in two other relationships and racked up a huge debt. When I moved in, we set up the rumpus room downstairs with a bed and some drawers. Knowing someone cared about my wellbeing was good, and I felt safe again.

✦

After a few months, Amy and I tried to give our marriage another go. It didn't take long before our relationship became rocky again because of financial pressures. I also realised that even though I still loved Amy, I wasn't in love with her and spent most nights sleeping on the lounge.

I had brought significant financial stress into the marriage. The debt I had created when I was in my manic stage was huge. I had little money to contribute to the household when I paid my weekly loan repayments. This caused several arguments.

I had hoped to get back on the mortgage, re-mortgage the house, pay off my loans, and contribute to everyday living costs. But no way was that going to happen after what I had put the family through. I had lost the house when I signed it over because of my mental health. I was comforted to know, though, that the kids would inherit it one day.

✦

Over time, things became a struggle with finances, making it hard to cover the bills. One day, while I was working in my graphic design role, I received a phone call from Amy. She wanted me to ask my boss for a pay rise. It hadn't been long since I received a pay raise, a company car and a petrol card. The boss is going to think that I am an ungrateful arsehole if I ask for another raise. Besides, I was getting pretty good money for the type of work I was doing—much more than I would get anywhere else.

Because I don't like confrontation, all I could think about was how the owner would react when I asked him for a raise. I imagined he would yell at me and say something degrading that would add extra weight to my already low self-esteem and confidence.

I didn't dare ask for another pay raise. So, I went home and told Amy I had asked him when I hadn't and that he would think about it. I felt terrible for lying.

✦

As time went on, my depression kicked in, and I saw a psychologist. She wanted to see me each week, which was hard, as I worked five days a week and often had to work overtime. Eventually, my boss got annoyed with me for taking time off and took me to the boardroom to discuss it.

I explained how I was feeling and why I was seeing the psychologist, but he didn't get it. He told me about his sports activities and that they keep him on track. He said I didn't need to see a psychologist; I only needed to take up a sport, and things would improve. Yeah, right, it's not that bloody simple. My mind exploded, and I told him to stick his job up his ass, packed up my stuff, and left.

Again, I wanted out of all this pain. The pain of the constant highs and lows, the pressure to find another job and the pressure of work. The thoughts of suicide instantly entered my head, but in the end, I went home first to see how things panned out with Amy. I was so scared of driving home.

How would I explain to Amy that I had quit my job because of all the financial stress we were experiencing?

It didn't go down too well when I first told her, which was totally understandable. When I explained the situation, she was more accepting.

✦

So, what the hell was I going to do now?

I still can't keep a job. I started doing some research on the Internet and noticed there were several jobs for security guards. Having spent many years training in martial arts, I thought that would be the perfect job. I could defend myself if I needed to. I didn't think for a minute that my dislike for verbal confrontation might be the worst thing I could do to myself.

After some research, I found an affordable security course. The course was relatively easy, and I made some friends along the way. We swapped numbers so that we could keep in touch after the course.

It took a while for the security licence to come through. Not long after, Max, a guy I did the course with, called and said he had a job lined up for me. The timing couldn't have been any better. I would work as a security officer, looking after two caravan parks. Max oversaw the security and needed an extra person, as it was safer for two security officers to work together.

We would walk the parks every one to two hours and spend the rest of our time in the camp kitchen. The shift went from 10 pm to 6 am and we drank coffee to stay awake. The problem I found with security was that I had too much time on my hands to think. That is not what you want when you are living with mental illness. I would be constantly ruminating about things that were happening in my life. The job wasn't the best for me in that way.

To top things off, the shifts were inconsistent, and I didn't know when I would work from one day to the next. I ended up having to find another job for my sanity and to look after my mental health. So, again, the job hunting began. I had to think long and hard about what I could do for work.

What could I do where maybe I could utilise my nursing training?

✦

While looking at job seeker sites, I saw an advertisement for a wardsman at a public hospital. I had no idea what was involved with this work, so I researched it and thought this might be the job for me. As always, I did well at interviews and landed the job.

The job started well; it was easy and was just what I was looking for. As a wardsman, I worked in many areas. One day, I would work in the surgical ward, x-ray, emergency department, morgue and various other locations around the hospital. Several other wardsmen were working in the hospital, which would be helpful during my learning process. Sadly, it was a clicky place to work and hard to fit in.

One of the sought-after jobs was working in the operating theatre. The primary task was to take people from preparation to theatre and then to recovery. This position involved cleaning the operating rooms and preparing them for the next operation. One of the best parts was assisting the surgeon in the operating room and holding up a patient's arm or leg. I loved working in the theatre, but the wardsmen didn't like new people threatening their position.

There was one wardsman who took a dislike to me. His shifts decreased after I started, and he blamed it on me. In retaliation, he constantly yelled at me for not doing things correctly, even though I was still learning. In one incident, he put saline bags onto a trolley without dates, which meant they had to be disposed of. He told the person in charge of the theatre that it was me, and I got into a lot of trouble. I couldn't bring myself to confront him or talk to my boss about it, as they had worked together for some time. I tried my hardest to fit in and become part of the team, but it was not working, and I always felt like an outsider. It also affected my self-esteem and confidence. Again, it was time to look for another job.

$$\bigstar$$

After searching the job seeker sites, I found an advertisement for an occupational therapy assistant. I applied for the job and was given the position immediately. This was the best job I've ever had. I loved it.

I worked with six lovely occupational therapists who were very pleasant. I enjoyed getting up in the morning and going to work. The therapists I was working with would visit older clients in the community. They would assess their living circumstances and what was needed to make their homes more accessible. This included aids for the toilet, rails, ramps and many other items. My job was to book all the appointments and install accessible items within the client's homes. I worked in this position for over a year. Even though I loved the job, I was still battling with mental health and struggling with it. I still didn't want to live and wanted out. There were still financial pressures and problems with Amy and me. Even though this may have contributed, it wasn't the main reason for my mental health challenges. I was still living with a mental illness that wasn't being treated.

✦

I had come to a point in my life where I couldn't keep living with the pain and looked for ways out—ways to end my life. This felt different from all the other times. I had decided that this was what I needed to do, and nobody would stop me. The weird part is that I was happy and content with my decision.

I did so much research on the Internet, trying to find ways you could end your life without pain. I had even created a spreadsheet on my work computer. I would hate to think what my work would have thought if they had reviewed my Internet history. After weeks of researching the Internet during my lunch breaks, before and after work, I couldn't find anything that didn't involve pain. Then, I reflected on what I had learned while nursing.

Having worked as a nurse ended up being a curse for me, as I knew too much about medications. After researching a few of my medication books, I eventually worked out a way that I could take my life with no pain at all. I could fall into a coma and die.

My mental health was declining more each day. I tried to seek help, but apart from a psychologist, I didn't know what other services were available to help me. I saw a psychologist, but it was too late, as I had already decided to go.

✦

I had my daughter's birthday coming up, and the last thing I wanted to do was to take my life too close to her birthday. So, I waited for a few more weeks. Even though it was still too close to her birthday, all I wanted was out, and I couldn't wait any longer. It was too painful living in my head. I thought the kids would be better off and happier not having me in their lives. How very wrong I was.

I talked to Amy about how I felt a few nights beforehand. I told her I didn't want to live anymore. But I didn't share that I had made plans, as I didn't want her to call an ambulance and end up back in the hospital.

That might have been a good time to call the ambulance and get me to the hospital. However, I did not blame Amy for not assisting me, as she had no idea I had a plan. Mental health and suicidal thoughts are hard to understand unless you have lived it or are living it yourself. Most people don't know what to do or say in that situation. Many times, suicide is unpredictable. I feel that nobody should be blamed or blame themselves for not being able to identify and stop someone from trying to take their life.

✦

This led me to my major suicide attempt in October 2019.
The following chapter carries on from the prologue at the beginning
of this book.

Chapter 13

Survival

For three days, I lay on the beach, unconscious and in a coma, semi-hidden in the sand dunes. I don't know what happened when rescuers found me.

After I got through the anger of being found, I located the surf lifeguard who rescued me. I asked about who found me that day so I could thank them and ask if they could fill me in on some details.

A lady saw me laying in the sand dunes on her daily beach walk. She wasn't too concerned on the first day. When I was in the same position on the third day, she alerted the lifeguards, concerned that something was seriously wrong. The lifeguards drove along the beach to my location in their four-wheeler.

I had tried to position myself far away from any houses or lifeguard towers, hoping that I would be dead before anyone found me. When the lifeguards got to me, I was severely sunburnt and had minimal vital signs. The lifeguard called the ambulance and tried to keep me alive until they arrived.

I later found out that one-twentieth of what I took would have killed a horse.

How was I still alive? How did someone find me ten minutes before I would have died when I had been laying there for three days?

I have never been religious, but after surviving against all odds, I feel that there must have been some higher power looking out for me. If there wasn't, I wouldn't be here. I was given another chance at life.

Sadly, my daughter was able to fill me in on a few things that happened after I was found on the beach that day. Lily said they heard someone had found me and was waiting at the hospital for the ambulance. I don't know where she was in the hospital, but she said that she saw them rushing along a corridor, cutting my clothes off. A paramedic was on top of me, performing CPR. Later, when I found out they had cut off my clothes, I was not happy, mainly because I lost my favourite jacket.

From what I understand, my heart had stopped between the beach and the hospital resuscitation rooms a few times. I was intubated and put into an induced coma even though I had been in a coma for three days before arriving at the hospital.

I don't know how long I was in the intensive care unit. But I will never forget the trauma, confusion, guilt and anger when I was woken up from the coma. My kids and Amy were at the end of the bed when they woke me up. They didn't know whether I was going to be a vegetable or if I was going to wake up at all. They were obviously distressed.

It took me quite some time to wake up. The first thing I remember was bright lights, like someone driving towards me with car headlights on full beam. I thought I must be in heaven or wherever you go in your next life. It was both scary and euphoric.

After a while, my vision adjusted, and I noticed some figures standing at the end of my bed. I heard a voice saying my name and telling me I was in the hospital and to open my eyes.

Was this an angel?

Once my vision was clearer, I noticed my kids standing at the end of the bed.

How did they end up in heaven with me? Where am I? What has happened?

After a bit more time going in and out of consciousness, I slowly started comprehending what people were saying around me.

I had tried to take my life, and I survived.

I felt a tremendous amount of anger rush over me.

How was I found? Why the hell am I still alive?

✦

I wanted to apologise to my kids, but I couldn't talk. As much as I tried, my brain wasn't communicating with my mouth. The nurse beside my bed saw I was agitated, upset and frustrated because I was struggling to communicate with my children.

The nurse asked me if I wanted to write on paper what I was trying to say to them. Due to not being able to speak, I managed to nod to say yes, and she got me a pad and a pen. This is when I noticed I was tied to the side of the bed. They had to untie me to write.

I could barely hold the pen and couldn't remember how to write. My brain was not communicating with my hand.

I slowly started communicating with the nurses and my kids as time passed. I remember needing to pee so badly. When I told the nurse that I needed to pee, she said that I had a catheter in and could pee whenever I wanted. I couldn't feel that I had a catheter in and thought that I was going to pee all over myself.

Eventually, I couldn't hold on and went. I thought I had peed all over the bed, but it went into the bag.

How did I know?

My daughter said, *Dad, I can see you going to the toilet.* She was watching my bag fill up at the side of the bed. I can laugh at it now, but I was so embarrassed then.

✦

The photograph on the next page shows me in the intensive care unit in October 2019.

There is help out there, and there is hope; you are loved.

This is not the place you want to go.

✦

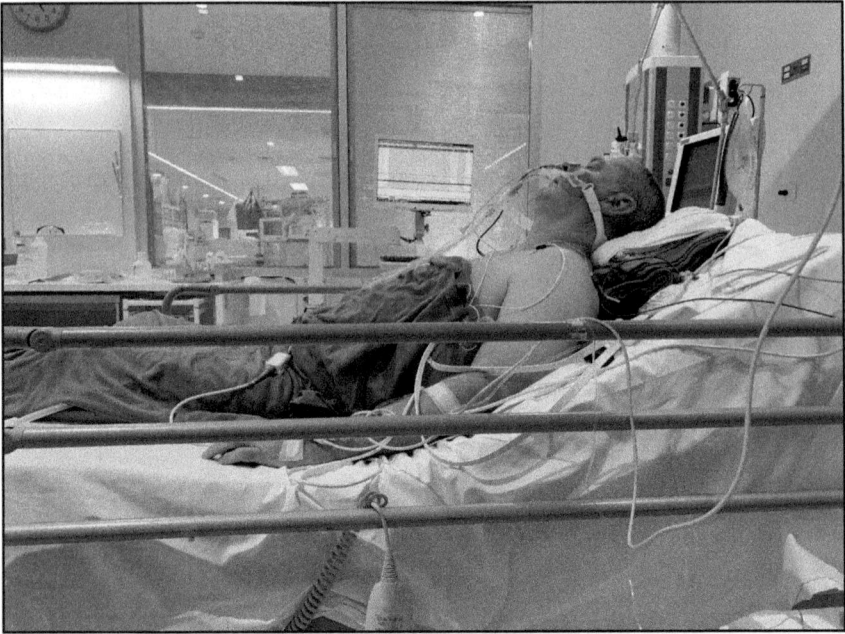

[Photograph by Lily.]

Intensive care unit—October 2019

This photo of me used to feel like a scar; painful, raw and hard to look at.

It captured a moment in time when I thought there was no way out, when I nearly lost my battle to stay alive.

But over time, I have come to see it differently.

Now it is a reminder.

A reminder to reach out before things get that dark.

A reminder that I do not have to carry everything alone.

There is always help, and there is always hope.

If you are struggling, please know that you are not alone.

There is strength in asking for support, and there is no shame in needing it.

✦

As I became more alert in the intensive care unit, I noticed I had tubes and wires coming out everywhere. I don't think there was one hole in my body that didn't have something in it. My nose hurt, which was aggravated, and I had to get it out. At first, I thought it was oxygen prongs, but after I started pulling it out, I knew it wasn't. I had been pulling out the feeding tube that was going into my stomach. The nurse was quite angry with me and said that she would have to reinsert it.

✦

There was one thing that happened when I was in intensive care that was quite embarrassing, and I found it very invasive. I had a rectal catheter coming out of my ass. The nurse informed me it was going to have to come out. When the nurse pulled it, it felt like the catheter was the size of a house, and it truly hurt. I could feel so much pressure that I told the nurse that when she pulled it out, I was going to explode and shit everywhere. She said that it was okay and that they had everything in place. Well, famous last words, my shit exploded everywhere and all over them. They couldn't say I didn't give them a warning.

✦

As time passed, most things became disconnected from my body, and I needed to use the toilet. There was no way I was going to poo in a bowl on my bed. So, I asked the nurse if I could use the toilet. After some convincing, she got a walking frame, put it by the bed, and said she would return in a few minutes to help me. Now, I was an impatient person.

Stuff it. I will try to do it myself. What could go wrong?

I managed to get myself up onto the walking frame but felt faint and that I was going to pass out. I sat back down on the bed and then tried again. Well, I didn't get very far as I was still connected to the drip, among other things. When the nurse came back, she wasn't impressed.

I refused a wheelchair, so the nurse assisted me to the toilet with the walking frame, and it took some time to get there. My brain was having a few issues talking to my legs, and I had little strength to walk, but I was determined. I was experiencing quite a bit of pain on my walk to the toilet that I hadn't experienced while lying in bed. I couldn't use my left arm, my chest and stomach hurt, and I had a weird sensation in my right leg. Plus, my face hurt because of severe burns from three days in the sun.

I had to pass the nurse's station on my way to the toilet. When I looked over, I noticed a nurse who was the mother of one of my daughter's friends. I had been to her house numerous times as the kids grew up, and she was Amy's close friend. She and her husband had turned on me when Amy and I had separated two years earlier. They would ignore me in the street and wouldn't acknowledge that I was there. They would even glare at me.

Well, she did the same thing to me in the intensive care unit. As I walked past the nurse's station, we made eye contact, so I said hello. She just glared and then looked away. This is when you need a familiar, friendly face to help you get through. Not only was she rude to me, but she was also nasty to my mother, who called from New Zealand. My mother called to check up on how I was doing, as you would when your son has tried to take his life. She initially refused to put her call through.

✦

The time had come for me to leave the intensive care unit. I didn't know where the doctors would transfer me.

Was I going to a regular ward to recover or to a psychiatric ward?

The psychiatric ward it was. A place I knew very well. I was put into a wheelchair and given a couple of vomit bags by the wardsman, and off we went. By the time I got to the ward, I had filled up both vomit bags. I was extremely sick, shaky, and sore. I was wheeled straight through the main area of the ward, where all the patients were sitting watching television. As I was passing them, I was filling my third vomit bag. Well, hello everyone, I'm home.

Having stayed in the ward many times, I thought I knew what I was in for. However, this would be the most horrific stay I've ever experienced. I was so sick that I ended up sleeping for the first day and through the night. I only left my bed to go to the toilet. The following day, I woke up with the most excruciating pain. I had severe pain in my left arm, couldn't move my wrist or fingers, and the back of my right leg was hurting like a bitch.

Most nurses on the ward received training in mental health. However, they could not handle the injuries I sustained from the suicide attempt.

Why was I sent to the psychiatric ward with the serious injuries that I had?

I guess the risk of me trying to take my life again made the ward a safer place to be.

After some time of crying in pain and not wanting to leave my room, the nurses called in a doctor to assess my injuries. The doctor started with my left arm. He told me I had a dropped wrist and that it may be because of a crushed nerve from laying on it for three days. My wrist and fingers hung down. It was like they weren't even connected to my body. It is very frustrating and concerning when you look at your wrists and fingers, and no matter how hard you try, they won't move.

To top things off, the pain in my arm was severe, which was weird considering I had numbness from the elbow down. The outside of my arm had little feeling, but the inside hurt like hell. The doctor called in the resident physiotherapist. I was fitted with a brace that kept my wrist straight, hoping I would eventually regain the feeling and use of my wrist and fingers. I also had no feeling on the left side of my body where I had been laying on my arm.

The doctor organised an ultrasound of my arm to check for blood clots. Sure enough, I had a blood clot in my arm just below my shoulder. I was given daily stomach injections of Clexane. Shit, they were painful. It wasn't the injection, but more the stinging from the fluid. I was so anxious whenever the nurse came into my room with the needle that I would have a panic attack.

The other thing causing significant pain was a pressure injury on the back of my thigh, which was the size of a saucer. There was also a decent-sized pressure injury on the back of my calf muscle. They had to be cleaned and dressed daily, making it difficult to shower. These pressure injuries worsened over time, and if they got any deeper, there was a chance of losing my leg.

Being in the psychiatric ward was not pleasant at the best of times. Having painful injuries at the same time made it an absolute nightmare. In saying this, I stress that the psychiatric ward is the safest place to be for anyone who is acute and at risk of harming themselves or others.

✦

I made a couple of friends while in the psychiatric ward. One of them was the mother of one of my children's friends—a lovely person. Having her as a friend and someone to talk to while in the hospital was great. My stay would have been much harder if it hadn't been for her. I was also fortunate to make friends with another lady who looked after me. She would talk so much that you couldn't get a word in. We would have our meals together and become good friends.

On the third day of being on the ward, I was called into a room to meet with the psychiatrist. This made me so anxious.

Why did he want to meet with me? What was he going to do with me after such a horrific attempt on my life?

When I entered the room, Amy was sitting on a chair opposite the psychiatrist.

What was she doing here?

We hadn't spoken since before the suicide attempt.

I sat on a chair, and the psychiatrist started the conversation. He revealed Amy didn't want me back in the house and that I had to find somewhere else to live.

This is crazy!

I have no money, am most likely out of a job and have nowhere to live. Life was getting worse.

How could she do this to me when I am at my most vulnerable?

I wanted to die. I was so upset that I couldn't even look at Amy.

How could she do this to me?

As time went on, I understood the way Amy was feeling.

How could you live with someone who constantly wants to take their life?

You would always be on edge and anxious, wondering when it would happen again.

The psychiatrist said he would organise an appointment to see the local social worker to arrange accommodation for discharge from the hospital.

Well, the social worker was hopeless, to say the least. He must have got his qualification out of a cereal packet. We discussed my needs at the first meeting and focused on accommodation options. The social worker said he would do some research and meet with me again in a couple of days.

Well, those days turned into two weeks, and the places he found were some of the worst places you could have ever seen. They were well-known for drug dealers, people with addiction and criminals. The female tenants would even sleep with the manager to pay the rent.

How was a person having depression and anxiety supposed to live in those conditions?

I would have been living in constant fear that something was going to happen to me.

✦

Things were looking bleak. I knew that if I were released in my current mental state, I would most certainly lose my life. I only had a few days before I was released when I met a lovely young woman who would change everything for the better. She was a mental health peer worker who worked at the hospital.

A peer worker is a person with lived experience in mental health who shares their recovery journey. It was comforting to talk to someone who had been through similar things, if not the same, as you. Finally, someone who understood me.

The peer worker told me of a sub-acute unit that was an hour's drive down the coast. It was a place where you could stay for three weeks and get the therapy you needed to assist with your ongoing recovery.

I feel everybody needs to attend a sub-acute unit following a stay in an acute psychiatric ward.

The sub-acute unit had a fantastic team of mental health workers and nurses, a peer worker, a dietitian, a psychologist, an occupational therapist and a social worker. You also had the option of seeing a psychiatrist during your stay. They were there to assist you in getting back on track with your mental health and help you integrate back into the community.

The idea of going there appealed to me. Until now, every time I was discharged from the hospital, I was left to my own devices. I was never referred to or told about any other services that could help me when I left the hospital. It was kind of like getting thrown out on the street. Your three-week stay is over now, piss off and good luck. Many people would either end up back in the hospital or take their lives due to not having services put in place when discharged.

I had nowhere to go when I left the hospital and would have lived on the street if I hadn't met the peer worker. The peer worker secured a room for me at the sub-acute unit. Once the psychiatrist approved my discharge, the patient transport ambulance drove me there.

✦

The sub-acute unit was nicer than I had thought it would be. I had my own room with an ensuite. There were two big television rooms, an art room, a dining room and even a little outdoor area in the middle of the building.

The other patients were friendly, which was a relief as I suffered severely from social anxiety. There was one familiar face, which was great. The friend I made in the psychiatric ward was there, and even though she would talk my ear off, it was comforting to know somebody.

Towards the end of my stay in the hospital, the pain in my left arm was increasing, and I was not getting any sleep. By the time I got there, the pain was unbearable. The first night of my stay was a nightmare, as I could not sleep at all.

I can't explain what nerve pain is like other than someone dragging a knife up and down your arm. To try to relieve the pain, I lay on my back, my side and every other position I could think of, but nothing worked. I ended up curling into a ball in the corner of the room, crying in pain.

Every half hour, the nurses would walk around to check that everyone was in bed, asleep, and safe. When the nurse came into my room and saw me curled up in the corner, crying in pain, she helped me to get dressed. She took me straight to the emergency department, only a five-minute walk away. Luckily, it was the middle of the night, and it wasn't busy, so I saw a doctor quickly. The doctor gave me some Endone and a medication called Lyrica, which was supposed to help with nerve pain. The nurse took me back to my room, and I lay patiently on my bed, waiting for the meds to kick in. But it didn't happen; the medication did nothing. It was a very long and painful night.

✦

Finally, the sun rose, and it was time for breakfast. Eating was challenging, as I couldn't use my left arm and needed help from a nurse. After breakfast, patients sat in the lounge room, and the therapy began. The mental health clinicians would take us through various therapeutic techniques to educate us on ways to help ourselves. Some therapeutic methods would work for some and not others, but everyone seemed to take something away that would be helpful. One person's journey through mental health may differ entirely from the person next to them.

For the first week of my stay, I could only sit in the morning sessions for ten minutes. The pain in my arm was extreme. I couldn't focus on what the clinicians were saying and would sit there in tears. To try to ease the pain, I was taking Endone regularly, but it wasn't working. I argued a lot with the nurses for more pain relief, but they kept saying that there was nothing more they could do for me.

The other thing I had to deal with was the pressure injuries on my leg, as they were getting worse each day. One day, I was taken into the medical room by two nurses to change the dressings on my leg. One nurse removed my dressings, and the other had to leave the room because it was so bad. It was large, deep, full of slough, and had a horrible smell. The nurses decided the wounds were too advanced for them to care for. They organised for me to visit the emergency department daily so that one of the doctors could treat them.

The daily visits to the emergency department had caused my anxiety to go through the roof. It was such a painful procedure, but if I wanted to keep my leg, I had to go. I waited for over an hour before a doctor swirled a big swab around the inside of the wound to remove the white slough. If that didn't hurt enough, they would cut away any dead skin around the wound. Sometimes, it wouldn't just be the dead skin they would cut off. It was so painful.

The unit was right next to a beautiful river and bushland. It was such a calming place to be. Once we had finished our morning therapy, we were allowed out of the unit to do whatever we wanted for the rest of the day. We just had to be back before they closed the doors at night.

Most of the other patients were smokers, so we would spend most of the day sitting across the road smoking one cigarette after another. The ironic thing was that the place we would sit to have a cigarette was on the edge of a cliff face. It was maybe a bit of a safety hazard for someone living with mental illness. Occasionally, we would go for a bush walk along the river or to the local cafe.

✦

I had been in the unit for a week when I had a checkup with the physiotherapist I saw in the psychiatric ward. They were concerned that nothing had improved with my arm, wrist and fingers. So, they put my arm in a plaster cast that went up over my elbow, and my wrist and fingers pointed upwards. They hoped that my wrist and fingers would stay upright when the cast was removed, rather than dropping downwards. Unfortunately, it was unsuccessful. Once the cast was removed, the physiotherapist scheduled an appointment with a nerve specialist for nerve conduction studies. This would help evaluate the extent of the nerve damage.

For those who haven't had a nerve conduction study, all I can say is that it is awful. The specialist has a prodder that has a strong electrical current running through it. They place the prodder on your arm and zap you to see if your nerve reacts. It would make your whole body jump.

When the specialist zapped the affected areas of my arm, wrist and thumb, there would be no reaction at all. The specialist confirmed that my arm and hand function may be permanently impaired because of nerve damage.

✦

After three weeks, the standard length of stay, I felt no different than when I first went in. Mentally, I was still in the same place as when I left.

My mother called me a few days before I was due to be discharged. I cried when I told her I couldn't participate in the programs for the first couple of weeks. I explained this was because of the severe pain in my arm and leg and that I still had nowhere to live. I was feeling lost, angry and hopeless, and I still felt like I didn't belong in this world.

Mum became extremely upset and angry with the hospital and called them to raise her concerns about my mental health. She told them it would not go well if they discharged me in a few days. I was called in to see the head nurse and social worker. They said they would extend my stay by another three weeks.

Shit, another three weeks.

I was so over the hospital by this stage, but I knew it was for my own good.

The head nurse was concerned about my mental status and safety, so she organised a psychiatrist to see me. It was to decide whether I was safer to stay in the sub-acute unit or if I needed to go back to the ward.

The psychiatrist was thorough. He must have spent at least two hours with me, reviewing my life from childhood until now. He said that the diagnoses I had to date were incorrect and that I had bipolar disorder. This matches the diagnosis that I received the first time I ever saw a psychiatrist, the diagnosis I didn't want to accept.

I saw several psychologists during the worst years of my mental health journey. I also received several diagnoses that were incorrect, with the two main ones being borderline personality disorder and situational depression. One thing I learned along the way is that it is hard for a psychiatrist to give the right diagnosis if you don't share all the important information about your life and what you have been experiencing. I'm saying that a good psychiatrist will ask all the right questions to get this information.

I was prescribed a new medication called Lamotrigine. I knew from experience that medication took around six weeks to kick in, but I noticed a change in my mood within a week. My suicidal thoughts had also reduced a little.

✦

After another two weeks in the hospital, I had enough and desperately needed to get out. I told one nurse I was feeling better and ready to go. This was even though I had been thinking of taking my life a week earlier. The nurse told me to speak with the social worker, who would then decide whether I was ready to leave.

The social worker wasn't convinced that I was well enough to leave and organised a meeting with the psychiatrist. He got me to fill out a K10, which evaluates psychological distress. I had previously completed many K10 forms. So, I knew how to fudge it to make it look like I was doing well, but not too well.

He asked me if I had somewhere to live. I told him that Amy said I could move back into the house until I found somewhere else. Luckily, they didn't check with Amy as I had made the story up. It was a complete lie to avoid having to stay in the unit. The psychiatrist agreed I was well enough for them to discharge me from the unit.

Finally, I was free, but where was I going to go?

At that stage, I had some money left in my bank account, so I bought a tent and stayed at a camping ground.

Chapter 14

Homelessness

The camping ground was great at the start; it was summer, and I felt like I was on holiday. The grounds had a toilet, shower block, a camp kitchen and everything I needed to survive. Thankfully, Mum was drip-feeding money to me to pay the ground fees and to buy food.

One night, while cooking my dinner in the camp kitchen, I met a lovely couple named Ben and Leah. We hit it off and became close friends, and I felt comfortable sharing my story with them. I told them everything I had recently gone through with my mental health and suicide attempt. They were understanding and non-judgemental.

A few days after meeting them, Ben came to my tent. He asked if I would like to pitch my tent on their site to have some company and save money. I was pretty excited by the offer and moved over that day.

It was a crazy, fun time staying with Ben and Leah. We would stay up to all hours of the morning, drinking and getting very drunk. Ben would constantly pay for the alcohol, would cook me dinners, and buy me KFC and other takeaway food. I had trouble accepting things from people and felt awkward, mostly because I thought I didn't deserve it. Ben said that most of his trip was funded by his father, who was quite wealthy and not to feel bad.

Ben was a keen surfer and would go surfing every day. When I told Ben I used to surf in New Zealand, he was excited and lent me one of his boards to surf with him. I had the cast removed from my arm while in the sub-acute unit and was given a splint to wear. It had steel rods in it to keep my wrist secure. Plus, it was made from wetsuit material that allowed me to go in the water. I was set.

I had been in the surf for only two minutes when the pain in my arm became unbearable. I couldn't paddle or put weight on my arm to get up on the board. I was upset as it was, but then I realised there would be several activities I couldn't do because of the damage to my arm. It was going to be a constant reminder.

When we were drunk one night, Ben suggested I get a bodyboard to return to the surf, as you only needed to use your legs. I agreed with Ben that it would be a great idea, but there was no way that I could afford to pay for one.

The following day, Ben and Leah disappeared for a while. When they returned, Ben pulled a brand-new bodyboard and flippers out of his car and gave them to me. I didn't know what to say. I thanked them profusely but felt I didn't deserve it and was guilty that they had bought it for me. That afternoon, Ben and I went surfing together. It was so much fun to be back in the water again.

Camping with Ben and Leah was enjoyable at the start. It was probably not good for my mental health, though, as most nights, I would go to bed comatose from drinking way too much. After a while, things took a turn for the worse. Leah didn't handle her alcohol very well and would get quite violent when she was drunk, not with me, but with Ben. She would scream at Ben so loudly that people would come out of their caravans and tents to see what was happening.

There were a couple of nights when Leah physically attacked Ben, and he had to call the police because he could not calm her down. I decided that moving my camping site would be a good idea to give Ben and Leah space to sort out their problems. I would visit them every two to three days to have a beer but wouldn't stay longer than a few hours.

They asked if I wanted to join them at the local tavern for a few drinks one night. I was pretty excited, as I felt lonely. We decided to keep our spending to a minimum and had some beers before we left. That wasn't the best idea, as we were all drunk before going to the tavern.

The tavern was packed; you could hardly move. It was rocking, and the three of us hit the dance floor. We were having fun until Ben disappeared and was gone for quite some time. Leah went to look for him and found him flirting and dancing with some young girls.

She came back to keep me company, but she was upset. Leah and I had fun dancing away, and then Ben came back. He took one look at us dancing together and disappeared again. Nothing was going on between us; we were dancing, but I think he thought more was happening.

While on the dance floor, a guy approached Leah and asked her to dance. They became quite intimate, so I thought it was time for me to get out of there before Ben returned and all hell broke loose. I went outside for a smoke. While outside, Ben came along looking for Leah. He asked me where she was, and I told him I had no idea. He just glared at me and went back inside. I decided it was time for me to return to the camping ground.

There were some strong winds when I returned to the camping ground that night. My tent had blown down, and all the poles were snapped in half. It was freezing cold, and I had nowhere to sleep, so I slept in my car that night.

I had run out of money and couldn't afford another tent or food. I didn't want to ask Mum for more money as she had already given me too much, so I checked out of the camping ground. I slept in my car for some time, but didn't tell my mum or my kids, as I didn't want them to worry about me. As I had done in the past, I started searching the bins outside fast-food restaurants for leftover food. It's amazing what you can find.

✦

My mental health hit rock bottom again. I was so depressed that I wanted to die. I had been stockpiling my medications, so I had enough to finish things off if I needed to. I didn't think I would end up in this mental state again.

I headed down to the beach with my meds and a two-litre bottle of Coke. I sat in the dunes as I had previously done and was about to down the medications when my phone rang. It was my daughter. Suddenly, I had a rush of emotions.

What was I doing? How could I do this to my kids again?

I burst into tears and told my daughter what was going on, that I needed help, and needed to go to the hospital. I agreed to drop my car at their house, and she agreed to give me a lift to the hospital. This was the first time that I had gone to the hospital voluntarily without an ambulance.

Because of my history of suicide attempts, I didn't have to wait in the emergency department for long. They took me to a room to see the mental health team. The head psychiatrist came and saw me and decided I wasn't safe. He said he would put me in the PECC unit and would be back shortly with some paperwork.

While the head psychiatrist was gone, another psychiatrist came into the room and said that I was okay to go home.

This is crazy!

I was suicidal and was told by the head psychiatrist I was being admitted. I thought that the two psychiatrists must have talked with each other and decided I could go.

Go where?

I was living in my car and had no money to buy food. Luckily, the head psychiatrist came back before I was discharged. The other psychiatrist wasn't even supposed to be there and shouldn't have discharged me. Things could have gone terribly wrong.

While in the PECC unit, a social worker came to see me. Now, this person knew what they were doing. They made a few phone calls and found me a place at a local men's refuge where I could stay for three months. The vacancy wouldn't become available for a few weeks, but they found a temporary place to stay.

After a week, I was released from the hospital and moved into the temporary place. It was great; I had a room with a king-size bed and a freezer full of frozen meals. It was a comfortable place to stay; it had a small lounge, bedroom and an ensuite bathroom. There was also a fridge, freezer and microwave.

It wasn't long before I moved to the refuge. It was a strange setup. You went through a security gate with a six-foot fence and then through another security door leading into a private courtyard. There were six separate units. It ended up being quite a scary and confronting place to live. Except for one, the tenants in the other five units had just been released from jail. Two of them were violent, and they were all either drug dealers or users. Most nights, I couldn't sleep as one tenant was dealing drugs in front of my unit.

✦

During my time at the refuge, I got sickness benefits. It wasn't much money, but it helped. I didn't have to apply for jobs like I would have if I had been on JobSeeker financial support.

A mental health nurse from a community mental health service would visit me regularly. When I moved out, she continued to see me for over a year. It wasn't long before the nurse noticed significant problems with my short-term memory and concentration span. I was forgetting everything we had talked about during our visits. I would even get lost mid-conversation. The nurse suggested it would be a good idea to see my doctor. This was so I could get a referral to a neuropsychologist and have some tests done to discover what was happening.

✦

The appointment with the neuropsychologist came around quickly. Because of COVID-19, we couldn't be in the same room. So, she set up a computer in a room where I would be by myself and did the testing through the computer and a microphone.

The test was quite confronting and draining. With one question, she asked me to name as many animals as possible within two minutes, and I named three. That's when I knew that there was something wrong. I was eventually diagnosed with a hypoxic brain injury from a lack of oxygen to the brain. This happened because I lay on the beach in a coma for three days.

The neuropsychologist referred me to a brain injury service to help me with strategies for how to live with a permanent brain injury. It took me a long time to come to terms with the fact that I even had a brain injury. Many times, I thought I would be better off dead than living with what I had done to myself.

Because of the severity of my brain injury, my mental health nurse encouraged me to apply for a Disability Support Pension. This was because I was told that there was a high chance I would never study or work again. The nurse helped me fill out the application forms. We submitted them along with documentation from the doctors, psychiatrists, the hospital, the brain injury service, and other specialists I had seen.

✦

During my stay at the refuge, I constantly got calls from debt collectors regarding my bank and car dealership loans. I was way behind in payments and had no way to pay. I had no choice, but to go bankrupt. This was confronting as it would make it hard to get credit or loans for the rest of my life. I had no option.

Looking back now, it was for the best that I couldn't access money. I would have probably got myself into more debt while I was experiencing hypomania. I lost my car because of bankruptcy. It was timely, as my gearbox had failed, and I was facing a $5,000 repair bill.

✦

My three-month stay at the refuge was ending. The person who oversaw my accommodation made an appointment for me to meet with the manager of a local boarding house. Legally, they couldn't put me out on the street; they had to have something else in place. There was no way that I could afford to rent. Seriously, who was going to have me as a roommate with my mental health history and no job.

I met with the manager of the boarding house at her office. She was a scary and abrupt lady that you wouldn't want to get into an argument with. She wanted me to complete the tenancy paperwork before we drove down to look at the accommodation. I would have rather looked at the accommodation first but followed her request to avoid confrontation.

I had never seen or heard of a boarding house before and was shocked. There was a long hall with about ten rooms on each side. There was a small kitchen and a tiny lounge. When she showed me my room, I almost fell over, as it was the size of a small bathroom. It had a kid's single bed, which was unsuitable, as it was about four feet long, and I was six feet tall. The bed went from wall to wall, and a set of drawers was only two feet from the bed.

She introduced me to a couple of the tenants who were questionable—more criminals and people dealing drugs. The cost of staying in the boarding house was ridiculous. You would pay nearly the same price for renting an entire unit. This would have used all my sickness benefits, and I would have struggled to pay for food. I had signed all the paperwork for this place and felt like I couldn't pull out, as I was desperate. I told the lady I would call her later that day with a date I would move in.

As I was walking back to the train station, I lost it and broke down in tears. I could not live in that place; I would rather live on the street. When I got to the train station, I called Mum, as she wanted to know how it went. I could hardly talk; I was in a mess. I told her I couldn't do it anymore. I said I had a brain injury, limited use of my arm and was going to live in a shoe box. I was broken.

Mum said she would call the refuge to see if they could extend my stay for a few months. She called the refuge and explained my predicament and the complications that may occur if they get me to move out. Thankfully, they were empathetic and agreed to extend my stay for a couple more months to give me time to organise more suitable accommodation. Only a few weeks later, I was approved for the Disability Support Pension. That was the best news I had received in a long time, as I could now move into my own unit.

✦

I faced a couple of problems when looking for a place to live. I didn't have a rental history and could no longer work.

How was I going to compete with other rental applicants?

Thankfully, John from the refuge and my mother came to the rescue. John gave me a great reference, and my mother offered to be a guarantor to ensure my rent would be paid.

After a lot of searching, I found a lovely one-bedroom unit only a block from my favourite beach. The real estate agent was kind enough to let me prove myself as a tenant. I moved into the unit within a couple of weeks with financial help from Mum.

Moving into my own unit was like a breath of fresh air and a weight off my shoulders. Not only did I finally have a roof over my head, but I could now focus on my mental health recovery. I like to call it ongoing recovery, as I know that after having been diagnosed with bipolar, I would never be fully recovered. However, I could work towards reducing the severity and frequency of my condition.

Chapter 15

The battle begins

Securing accommodation was a small step towards my ongoing recovery. It was going to be a real challenge. Not only would I have to work on my mental health, but I discovered that my brain injury was a lot worse than I thought.

My long-term memory wasn't too bad, as I could remember many things from my past, but my short-term memory was completely gone. I would forget everything. There wouldn't be a day when I left my unit that I would forget my keys and lock myself out. I think that every second day, I would visit the real estate to borrow their spare keys and get back in. I had to keep a spare key with my neighbours, but even then, I would forget that I had given them a key.

I would put food in the oven and forget it was there until I could smell it burning, then forget to turn it off. I would walk into a room and completely forget why I went there. I constantly lost things around the house and forgot to turn things off. There was even one time I left the shower on all day.

Grocery shopping was a nightmare. I would leave the house, get halfway up the street, and forget where I was going. Sometimes, I forgot my phone and wallet when I reached the supermarket. As for getting the food that I needed from the supermarket, it never happened. When I made a list, I would leave the list at home. I can't recall the number of umbrellas or hats that I lost.

Sometimes, I sat down to have something to eat or sat down at the beach. I would leave behind any item that wasn't connected to me or in a pocket. This included my wallet and phone. I would constantly cancel my bank cards. The problems I was having with my short-term memory were causing me anxiety, depression and frustration and left me in tears.

My mental health nurse, Sally, was becoming concerned about the issues I was having. She explained that the issues were because of my brain injury and were affecting my mental health and daily living activities. Sally suggested we apply for the National Disability Insurance Scheme (NDIS). This service would enable me to receive more help with my daily struggles. We spent the next session filling out the paperwork and submitting it with my medical information.

While waiting for the NDIS to be approved, Sally hooked me up with a mental health rehabilitation service. Having Sally and John from the rehabilitation service made for a great team. They did wonders for my mental health and referred me to the other services I needed.

✦

One thing that I learned through my ongoing recovery is that you can't get any better unless you want to help yourself. I hated being told that by mental health specialists, but it is true. Whenever I saw a mental health clinician in the past, I would expect them to have a magic cure. Mental health clinicians don't have a magic cure. They can, however, give you the therapeutic tools and guidance that can assist you with your ongoing recovery. I found the only way to improve my mental health was by using the therapeutic tools provided by the clinician and putting them into action.

Not every technique the clinician shares will resonate with you, but the ones that do will help. It was the same with psychiatrists. I used to think that when they supplied me with medications, my mental health issues would go away.

This is not the case either. Yes, it takes the edge off what you are experiencing. However, you still need to talk therapy combined with the medications to move forward. In saying all this, it is tough to work on helping yourself when you are in a very dark space. The important thing for me was to stay as safe as possible until the dark space became lighter, and I was ready to move forward.

The other thing I learned is that you don't get better overnight. Things are going to take time. You need to take small steps, one step at a time. I had spent the last eight to ten years struggling with my mental health, and it would not go away that easily. I needed to fight and fight hard.

My NDIS was approved, and I could finally access some disability services. I was assigned a NDIS support coordinator who would help me find the services to meet my needs and help improve my current living situation. By the time the NDIS got approved, I had become isolated and had shut myself off from society. I would only leave the house occasionally to walk along the beach. The beach is my calming place, which is ironic since I tried to take my life there.

After a while, I stopped going for beach walks, and my isolation worsened. I felt like people were looking at me, judging me and that I had *crazy person* written across my forehead. I felt like people could see that I had a brain injury.

The first thing my NDIS support coordinator focused on was setting up regular support. This included help with my everyday activities, which were compromised because of my brain injury. She met with a lovely lady from a disability support service. She was a support worker who would visit my unit four times a week.

The support worker assisted me around the house, took me on walks, accompanied me for a coffee, and helped with grocery shopping. She helped me set up whiteboards to track the appointments I was missing. We put post-it notes around the unit as reminders to turn off the stove, shower, etc. We even made a list of things to take with me before I left the unit, such as my wallet, keys and phone. We also set up medication boxes, so that I wouldn't forget to take my medication. Who knows where I would be today if I didn't have this service available.

Another service she organised was to see an occupational therapy specialist for brain injury. The therapist was great. We would work together on different techniques to help me remember things. This included setting reminders on my phone and utilising the whiteboards set up by my support workers. She was doing a great job, but I would forget to put things into my phone or use the whiteboard when she wasn't there. I persisted and tried my hardest to implement her techniques. I didn't have the heart to tell her that when she wasn't there to remind me, I would forget everything she had taught me.

Eventually, the therapist said that she would discharge me and explained that she had done all she could. She said I could contact my NDIS support coordinator and get her back should I need more help. I got her back for a refresher, but struggled to remember when she wasn't there.

✦

There were a few other things affected by my brain injury besides the short-term memory loss. My concentration span was severely affected. I used to be able to draw and paint for hours on end, but now I only have a concentration span of around ten minutes. My concept of time has also changed. I can't remember if I talked to someone yesterday or a month ago.

This affects my relationships with friends and family. I recently lost a friend because he hadn't heard from me for so long and gave up on me. My mother sometimes gets upset because I haven't called her for a while, but in my mind, I was talking with her yesterday. My patience has also deteriorated. If I wait in line for more than a few minutes, I get irritated and leave.

One of the most frustrating things is my inability to read and remember movies I've just watched, or even recall the movie's name. I struggle to retain information. I would read the first page of a book, and then when I got to the second page, I would forget the first page. I remember telling my support worker I had watched a good movie the night before. When she asked me what the movie was about or the name of the movie, I couldn't tell her.

My brain injury improved a little in the first year, but it has stayed the same since, and I still struggle in my everyday life. The brain injury specialists initially said it may improve a little over the first year, which it did. However, it would be something that I would have to live with for the rest of my life. The therapist said there was nothing more that could be done other than putting strategies in place to make it easier to live with the injury. That has been difficult to come to terms with. I have done extensive therapy with my psychologist to accept that I have a permanent brain injury.

$$\blacklefthalf$$

After living in isolation for quite some time, I knew I had to get out into the community without relying on my support workers. Being isolated was bringing back my depression, and there was no way that I was going back to living with suicidal thoughts again. I had to help myself as nobody would do it for me.

My support workers were taking me out regularly, and my social anxiety was reduced a little. I could go out into the community on my own more often. One day, when I met with Pete from the rehabilitation team, he brought a peer worker with him—she was a lovely person. She told me about a local men's group that had several members with a lived experience of mental health and had a significant Facebook presence. She explained it may be a good way to get out into the community without feeling judged.

That night, I checked the Facebook group and read the posts from other members. They seemed friendly, and you could attend any activities. They would meet at the beach twice a week for an early morning walk before work. I tried to take part in one of these walks.

Living with social anxiety made it difficult for me to attend. For the first couple of weeks, I would get up half an hour before the walk started and get dressed. I couldn't even make it out the door. There were several days when I would make it to the beach but didn't have the courage to walk over to where they would meet. Eventually, I went closer to where they would meet and watched from a distance to see if I could find them approachable. They seemed like pretty nice people. So, I thought I would bite the bullet and walk up to them, but I couldn't and walked past them. I followed them for a bit, but still couldn't get the courage to approach them.

I knew for my mental health that I had to make contact. So, I sat on the beach, hoping the group would return to where they started the walk. They did return, and finally, I got the courage to walk up and talk to the person leading the group. The guy was friendly, but I found it hard to make conversation. I would ask questions, and he would only give two-word answers. I was finding it awkward and was getting ready to bail.

After a few minutes, one of the other group members walked up and talked to me. He was very friendly and asked me lots of questions about myself. I felt comfortable. We had several things in common, including the same mental health diagnoses. We would become good friends.

Over time, I took part in activities with the men's group. We would go bowling, play golf, participate in trivia, and engage in other activities. The group's organiser owned a well-known burger bar, and the group would meet there once a month for a free burger and a beer. It was the best burger in town and was my favourite part of being part of the group.

I still suffered from social anxiety while attending the group. I had made friends with two people, and if they weren't at the monthly get together, I couldn't attend. It was too overwhelming, and I would be overcome with fear.

✦

After a while, I felt like my life had become mundane. When I wasn't with my support workers or attending the men's group, I would sit in the lounge watching television or in silence. Sitting in silence isn't good for somebody living with mental illness. It gave me time for racing thoughts and ruminations to take over my mind.

Racing thoughts are fast-moving, often repetitive, overwhelming and debilitating. If I worried about something insignificant, my head would turn it into a tsunami. For me, this was a common occurrence.

During one of my visits with my support worker, I was visibly upset and crying. I told her I was so lonely and was struggling. She suggested I get a kitten. What a great idea! I would like to have a companion. I knew I had to run the idea past my real estate agent. Well, that didn't go well. She said that no pets were allowed in the unit block, even if they were therapy pets. I was devastated, but thankfully, that was about to change.

One day, while walking along the beach, I ran into the parent of a child I used to coach soccer. He said that I was renting a unit that belonged to his mum.

What are the odds?

I told him about the issue I was having regarding getting a kitten. He agreed it wasn't fair and would talk to his mother, who would then call the real estate agent, which she did.

It didn't go down well with the real estate. As they saw it, I had gone behind their back. A few weeks later, I received a call from them stating that my application for a pet had been approved. I got a lovely kitten who became a great companion, and I no longer felt lonely.

✦

Even though I wasn't good at keeping jobs, I had worked my entire life and was struggling with the time I had on my hands. The silence was deafening, and the boredom was killing me. I decided that even though I had a brain injury and issues with my arm, there must be something out there that I could do. I wanted to work again and be able to support myself.

But what the hell do I do? Who is going to employ me?

I spent weeks researching and trying to think about what I could do to utilise my lived experience of mental health.

What about a mental health peer worker?

I knew that peer workers live with mental illness. Maybe the organisation that I would end up working for might be accepting of my brain injury and my mental health history.

I started researching what was required to become a peer worker. The main requirement was to complete a Certificate IV in Mental Health Peer Work through TAFE. Okay, now that could be a problem.

How was I going to complete TAFE?

After all, I was told that I would probably never study again. I couldn't even remember what I had done the day before or what I had read when I got to a book's second page. I was determined that I was going to give it a good go and fight my way through this injury and improve my mental health.

I ended up sending an application to TAFE. I included as much information as I could about my brain injury and my mental health, so they knew from the start. If they didn't think I was suitable, they could let me know sooner rather than later. A few days after submitting my application, I received a call from TAFE saying that I had been accepted into the course. The teacher said I would be an asset as a peer worker because of my lived experience.

I was excited, and finally, I had something to look forward to. I had also been accepted as a human being, not a crazy person who would be unemployable.

✦

Unfortunately, I didn't get off to a good start with the course. I would listen intently to what the teacher was saying, but when I went to write my notes, I forgot everything she had said. I couldn't retain any of the information.

The assessments were just as bad. I would search the Internet to find the required information. Before getting the information off the screen and onto paper, I would forget what I had just read. It would take me several days to complete an assessment, which should have only taken a couple of hours. Most days, I was in tears.

My assessments were piling up a month or two into the course, and I struggled. I had tried my hardest but felt defeated. I asked the head teacher if I could withdraw from the course. It was causing too much stress and anxiety, and I was feeling drained because of the pressure that I was putting on my brain. When the class was over, I couldn't function at all. My brain couldn't take any more.

The teacher said she didn't want me to give up and that she and TAFE would do everything possible to help me. The teachers sent me the PowerPoint slides and other information they discussed in class, so I didn't have to take too many notes. Because of COVID-19, the course was done online.

I made quite a few online friends as we went along. Two of these friends went out of their way to help me. They would send through their notes and some of their assessments. This was to give me an idea of how to set things out, not for plagiarism.

Along with the teachers and students, the occupational therapy brain injury specialist helped me with different techniques to help retain some of the information. It was still tough, and there were many days when I was ready to give up. But I was determined not to end up back where I had started. I was going to fight.

✦

My life had started getting better. I was getting help from the community mental health service, mental health rehabilitation, the occupational therapy brain injury specialist and my support workers. I had an entire team of support. I also attended the men's group, which occasionally got me out of the unit. If I didn't have my support team, I most likely wouldn't be where I am today.

Having so many appointments can be frustrating and overwhelming, as it takes up much of your life. I want to stress the importance of having a good mental health team behind you. They all have techniques and ways of helping with your mental health. There are things you can take from everyone in the team.

As mentioned earlier, though, there is no quick fix. No clinician or mental health worker has a magic solution to take away all your pain, stress, anxiety and depression associated with your mental illness. There is no magic pill. You need to participate and work on the tools and techniques that the mental health workers provide you.

As challenging as it may be, you will not move forward unless you are prepared to help yourself. But for me, I had to be ready. I found that when I was in my darkest place, I wasn't ready to help myself. I didn't have the strength. I couldn't use the tools and techniques the clinicians shared with me and put them into action. I had to focus, find some hope one day at a time, and keep fighting until I was ready.

I remember attending a couple of dialectical behavioural therapy groups. It is an amazing therapy for many types of mental illnesses. I was in no state of mind to take anything in. My mind was in a dark place. Based on what we had learned from each session, I didn't have the strength to do the homework. It wasn't until I attended another group later that I was ready. I had to keep fighting, survive and not give up hope because there is always hope.

Chapter 16

Loss of a child

While I was living in Australia, my mother was in regular contact with my eldest son, Jack, who was living in New Zealand. Mum and Jack had formed a close relationship, and Jack would regularly visit Mum. Mum was always there for him, through both the good and the bad, and would even help him when he was short of money.

Jack lived with mental health challenges but didn't have a diagnosis. When I look back now, I can see the similarities between Jack and me and feel that he may have been living with bipolar. Unfortunately, without a diagnosis, Jack would not have been getting the treatment he needed.

Two significant events happened in Jack's younger years.

The first was that his young sister became very ill, and his mother, Kate, spent many months looking after her in the hospital. Unfortunately, this added to Jack's insecurities.

The second was when his mother remarried, and it was around this time that Jack started having panic attacks. When he turned fourteen, he experimented with drugs and alcohol. He also spent most days at the local skate park, getting into all sorts of trouble.

Many people who live with mental illness will self-medicate with drugs and alcohol. I feel that this was what Jack was doing to cope. Even though self-medicating takes away the pain at the time, it makes things a lot worse in the long term.

When Jack turned sixteen, he was allowed to leave school, and his stepfather took him to get a tattoo. This would be the start of his addiction to tattoos. I know my mother gave his stepfather a fairly stern talking to. He told her he would never speak to her again.

Jack had a great friend named Levi, and they were as close as could be. Sadly, Levi had a debilitating disease called muscular dystrophy. They both went to live with the mother of one of their friends, and they would sleep on the floor in her house. Jack was great at looking out for Levi, but sadly, one awful morning, Levi didn't wake up. He had died in his sleep. I can only imagine the grief this must have caused Jack.

Jack moved into a boarding house and met his wife, Jane, the owner's daughter. Jane became pregnant around the time they met, and they were unsure if the child was Jack's. That never bothered them, and they loved him dearly.

Jack ended up getting a job at McDonald's, which he excelled at, and at last, he seemed happy. Unfortunately, this was not to last as they both did drugs and drank large amounts of alcohol. Jack ended up leaving McDonald's and moving to a country town where he worked as a farmhand. Later, Jack and Jane got married and had another two children together. Everything was going well for a while, but because of the financial issues, the drugs and alcohol, the marriage disintegrated, and eventually, they separated.

Jack found it hard to be separated from Jane, especially when trying to look after the kids by himself on the weekends. His mental health declined, and my mum and his boss became concerned. With some intervention, Jack went to the hospital for his safety. When they admitted Jack, Mum called me to tell me what was happening. I said to Mum that I would call him at the hospital over the weekend.

Jack hadn't been in the hospital long before he was released. The mental health specialist discharged Jack as they thought he was drug-seeking. This was even though it was obvious he was there for a decline in his mental health and suicidal thoughts.

After being discharged, Jack didn't know what to do and spent the night with some good friends. Jack told his friends what had happened at the hospital and how low he felt. So, they ensured he was safe, and he stayed with them for the night. They had a great night chatting, laughing and having a few drinks.

At the end of the night, Jack's friends set him up in the lounge with a blanket and pillow. They all went to bed, and Jack seemed in good spirits. When Jack's friends woke the following day, Jack was gone, and the blankets were folded and stacked nicely in the lounge. His friends thought he must have gone home for the day and that everything was okay.

That morning, my mum received a text from Jack, which was concerning. Mum tried everything she could to get hold of Jack but couldn't reach him. After several attempts and the concerning nature of the text, she called the police. They searched his property but couldn't locate him. Jack was in regular contact with my mum, and she was concerned about his mental health. There was no way she was going to lose Jack the same way she nearly lost me.

✦

Early Sunday morning, while I was asleep, I was woken up by my phone ringing. When I answered the phone, it was Mum—she was distraught. Mum asked me if my daughter, Lily, had arrived at my place. I was confused as I didn't understand why she was coming over, especially early in the morning. I knew something was wrong. I told Mum that Lily probably wasn't too far away and asked if she could tell me what was happening.

I would hear the worst five words I have ever heard, and they would tear my life apart.

Jack has taken his life.

I can't put into words the emotions that I experienced; it was horrific. A child should never die before their parent. I was lost and full of guilt.

How could I not be there to save my own child? Had he done this as he heard about all my suicide attempts?

I last saw Jack a year earlier, on my mother's seventieth birthday in New Zealand. We spent a few quality days together, creating memories I will cherish forever.

Because of COVID-19 restrictions in New Zealand, I could not attend Jack's funeral, which was devastating for us all. I would have got back in time but would have had to isolate when I got there until well after the funeral.

Because I couldn't get to the funeral, my three children, Amy and I, had our own beautiful service by the water to say goodbye. We decided to have it in the same spot where I had almost lost my life. Strange, I know, but I felt it held some significance. Lily put together a lovely wooden box with photos of Jack and me inside. She put an engraved plaque on the top of the box that included an engraving of one of Jack's favourite tattoos. It was heartbreaking and sad, but lovely at the same time.

Jack's funeral was live-streamed and recorded, and Lily watched it. I couldn't bring myself to watch his funeral live as I was too distraught, traumatised, and numb. Lily was upset and begged me not to watch the recorded video, as it was full of hate for our family. Mum also advised me not to watch it. I still haven't watched it today. I want to remember him for who he was, with a beautiful soul and a quirky sense of humour.

It took me two years to open the box Lily had given me to look at the photos of Jack. I have only been able to look at them a couple of times, as it is too painful. Jack has left a huge gap in all our lives.

Chapter 17

Ongoing recovery

With determination and hard work, my life began to improve. I was still having significant issues with my arm and the brain injury, but my mental health was improving. I had strategies in place, such as a wellness and safety plan. I kept it on my fridge, so I didn't have to hunt for it when I wasn't well.

When I was experiencing a decline in my mental health, I couldn't remember or think of distractions or ways to keep myself safe. Knowing my early warning signs, I can reach out to people who can help me and do some activities or techniques to reduce my stress.

Some aspects of my wellness and safety plan include my early warning signs, things that stress me, and ways to make my environment safer. I also have access to services and professionals who can help me, family and friends I can talk to and with whom I can share my plan. There are also things I can do to maintain my wellbeing, including things I do well and skills I possess, as well as short-term and long-term goals I can work towards.

I found that having these plans in place, combined with help from my mental health team, reduced my suicidal thoughts and stopped my suicide attempts. Over time, I have gone from having suicide as my safety blanket and trying to survive to wanting to live. I accept that I will still experience highs and lows throughout my life, but I feel safe that I have strategies to help myself.

I have learned through my journey that someone out there cares about you, whether it's a family member, a friend, a mental health professional, or even a stranger. After all, it was a stranger who saved my life.

Even though I didn't feel it then, people are not better off without you. I saw the damage that my suicide attempts did to my children. I will never forget seeing the trauma and sadness on their faces when I woke up in the intensive care unit. I can't imagine what it would have been like if I hadn't made it. It must have been so hard for them to live with a father who didn't want to live and was constantly trying to end things.

✦

My TAFE course was coming to an end, and I had to find an organisation where I could complete my placement. To finish the course, you had to clock up a certain number of hours of volunteering as a mental health peer worker. The thought of it was daunting, to say the least.

How was a person living with social anxiety going to achieve this?

I had given no thought to the fact that I would have to talk to several strangers every day.

What had I done? Why did I think I could be a peer worker?

My head was racing.

The head teacher of my course was such a lovely person—she was caring and showed empathy. She made it her mission to help find a placement for everyone in our class. Based on my lived experience, she helped me decide what mental health sector area I would like to work in. As an artist with lived experience of suicidal thoughts and attempts, we looked into art therapy and suicide prevention.

During my TAFE course, I got along well with a few of my classmates. There was one guy, Steve, whom I had only spoken to on the phone or via video, but it was as if we had been friends for years. One day, Steve called me to let me know he had landed a job as a mental health peer worker in suicide prevention for a large organisation. I was so excited for him.

The next thing he said was an enormous surprise and would completely change my life. Steve explained that the organisation was looking for an additional peer worker and that he had given them my name and contact details. He also told them I had a lot of lived experience with suicide and that I would be perfect for the role. Steve said they would like me to call them to organise an interview.

The following day, I called them to introduce myself and organise a time and date for the interview. I was so nervous. I must have sat there shaking for at least a few hours before I got the courage to make the call. With everything I had been through in my life, especially over the last few years, I had extremely low self-esteem and no confidence in myself.

How was I going to sell myself?

I made the call, and the people I talked to were lovely. I shared a little about my mental health journey and my ongoing recovery. They said that, given my lived experience, I would be well-suited for the position. So, we organised a date and time for the interview. They also asked if I could send my resume with a cover letter as soon as possible, before the interview.

After much searching, I found the resume I used for my last job interview. I only needed to make a few updates, and it was ready to send. The thing that I struggled with was the cover letter. In my past cover letters, I wrote about my graphic design skills and the attributes I could bring to the company.

But how the hell was I supposed to share my mental health attributes?

Well, I have had over ten visits to the hospital due to attempting to kill myself. I also have a brain injury that severely affects my short-term memory. I am perfect for this role, yeah right.

Unfortunately, there is a huge stigma around mental health and suicide. Many people don't understand unless they have experienced it themselves.

Most of the stigma comes from a lack of education about mental health and the way it is portrayed through the media. Many crimes are blamed on mental health. This makes people think that anyone living with mental health issues is a criminal, which couldn't be any further from the truth.

It was because of this stigma that I spent most of my life trying to hide my mental illness, especially from my employers. I felt that if they had found out, I wouldn't have got the job or been fired from the one I was working in. I had a secret that I had to hide from everyone except my closest friends and family.

You can imagine how confronting it was for me. I had to include my mental health in my cover letter when applying for a job as a peer worker. I decided to go for it and lay it all on the line.

After all, what did I have to lose?

✦

The interview went well. It was one of the best interviews I have had. The interviewers were lovely and empathetic to my situation. It only took a few days for them to let me know I had the position. I felt like I had won the lottery.

The position was three days a week. I still had to attend TAFE on the other two days and complete my assignments at night or on the weekends. Things were about to get hectic, and I was worried about how my brain would handle it. But I was determined to make things work, as it was a huge step in my ongoing recovery. I felt like I was part of society again.

✦

The first day of my new job arrived quickly. It was only a short walk from where I was, which was good, as I didn't have any transport at that stage. I got up early that morning, dressed, ate something, packed my bag, and headed off. I felt like a kid going to a new school for the first time. My anxiety was through the roof that morning, and the closer I got to work, the worse it got. I ended up vomiting three times along the way.

When I arrived at the building, I was shaking so badly that I couldn't go inside. Luckily, I was ten minutes early and could find a place to sit down and do some stress reduction techniques. I finally calmed myself down enough to enter the building. Everyone was so welcoming and friendly that I became less anxious.

One of the administrative team members showed me to the boardroom, where I would spend the next few days completing most of my training. I was pleasantly surprised when I walked into the room to find two other new peer workers who would train alongside me. What a relief. I wasn't on my own.

We had to go through all the company procedures as part of our training. It was difficult for me to remember everything due to my memory issues. The main thing was that I knew where all the procedures were located. This was so I could review them easily and find them should I need to refer to them.

Training went smoothly, but then the day arrived when I had to interact with some of the program's participants. Of course, it was my job to speak to the participants, but social anxiety and self-doubt crept in.

Are they going to like me? Am I going to be able to assist or help them with their mental health challenges in any way? Am I good enough?

Thankfully, I wasn't thrown into the deep end, and I would shadow the team leader for quite a few appointments. I would sit with the team leader and watch and learn how she worked with the participants. I would occasionally jump in when I felt it was appropriate. This also created anxiety. I was worried I would say something wrong, or the team leader might think I wasn't suitable for the position. After a few appointments, everything fell into place, and I felt comfortable taking on my own participants.

The program I was working in was suicide prevention and was predominantly run by peer workers. We would have the initial meeting alongside a clinician. Then, the clinician would only sit in with us every four weeks. The participants I was working with were acute, as they were experiencing suicidal thoughts or had attempted to take their life. I found out fast that my lived experience of suicide and my recovery journey were beneficial to them. I understood what they were going through, which was soothing for them.

Having someone working beside them who had been in that dark space and had made it through gave them hope.

The first few months of working with the participants and watching their suicidal thoughts subside were rewarding. Unfortunately, it took a toll on my mental health, and I experienced burnout. It wasn't so much having to relive my suicide attempts, but because I wasn't there to save my son, Jack. I couldn't detach from my participants when I went home at night, especially over the weekend. I would constantly be worried that when I returned to work the following week I might have lost someone. I took on everyone's pain as my own, and my mission was to save everyone.

There is one thing that I find difficult with being a peer worker. During the appointments, you tend to share some of the deepest and darkest parts of your mental health journey based on recovery. You don't over share, as you don't want to trigger anyone. You wouldn't even share some things you share with your friends or family.

In return, the participants share personal information, especially when they feel comfortable with you. This is where it gets difficult, as it's like you've built a friendship. When the participant is discharged, it can feel like you have lost a friend, as they have become a big part of your life. Much like the clinician, peer work is a professional service, and forming friendships with participants crosses the line. I get it, though. If you become friends, your work extends beyond working hours. If they returned to the service, it would be more of a friendship than a therapeutic professional connection.

After a while, I found my position in suicide prevention quite intense, and it was affecting my brain injury. When I got home at night, I couldn't do anything, but lay on the lounge. My brain could only take so much and was fried after eight hours of work. By the end of my third day, it would take me at least a day and a half to recover. I really wanted to work full-time and be able to come off the Disability Support Pension. I soon realised that I would not be able to. It took some time and therapy to come to terms with this.

After my second burnout, while working in suicide prevention, I knew I needed to move into something different. However, I still wanted to work as a peer worker. Just as I had decided to leave, a position became available within the same organisation. It involved working with participants with ongoing mental health challenges similar to mine. There was still an element of suicide prevention, but it was not as intense and as frequent as my current position. I am still only working three days a week. I have spread out my days by recommendation of my brain injury specialist to allow my brain to recover.

✦

So, where am I at today?

I still experience hypomania and depression now and then because of living with bipolar and other mental health diagnoses. They are less frequent and nowhere near as intense as they once were. I have strategies in place should my mental health deteriorate. I still have problems with my short-term memory, concentration and concept of time.

While writing this book, I underwent additional cognitive assessments, which were not particularly positive. Due to a recent decline in my brain injury, which isn't common with a hypoxic injury, I also had an MRI of the brain, which shows cerebral small vessel disease (CSVD). It is a relatively common neurological disease in older adults. The disease includes various conditions that cause damage to blood vessels in the brain. It causes stroke and dementia, gait problems and mood disturbances. There is no cure for CSVD, but you can delay complications via lifestyle changes and medications used to control blood pressure and lower cholesterol.

The brain injury and CSVD combined are not a good mix and don't have a good outlook. I am learning to live with them, adopting a healthier lifestyle, and moving forward the best I can. I have also reduced the number of days I work.

I am a much happier person now who wants to live. I have been free from suicidal thoughts since the start of 2020 and have no desire to go back to that space ever again. Should my brain take me there, I have a safety and wellness plan in place, along with a list of people and services I can reach out to.

✦

Why did I write this book?

Why did I want to share so much personal information about myself, especially when people would judge me?

Well, there are two main reasons.

The first reason is to give people an insight into what it is like to live with mental illness and not want to be alive.

Living with mental illness is not a choice. I don't want to be this way, and it is something that will not go away overnight. Being told to *take up a sport*, that *there are people worse than you in this world*, or *to get over it* are not helpful things to say to someone trying to recover or survive the pain of mental illness. It invalidates someone's pain and suffering.

Understanding mental health can be complicated if you haven't experienced it yourself. I hope that reading this book will help reduce the stigma and provide more insight and understanding.

The second and most important reason for sharing my story is to give people who are living with mental illness hope. Through all adversity, there is a light at the end of the tunnel.

I hope my story will give people the strength to fight through the darkness. Remember, it won't happen overnight, but it will happen by taking small steps, one step at a time. You are loved.

[Photograph by Paul Anthony. Location: Kiama Downs, NSW]

✦

The path to hope is taken one step at a time.

With each small step forward, you move closer to the light.

✦

Seeking help

If you or someone you love needs help, remember you are not alone. There is always someone who can help.

Below is a non-exhaustive list of services you can contact.

Use them as a starting point if you need help.

National services:

Emergency Services—Police, Fire, Ambulance: Call 000

Beyond Blue: https://www.beyondblue.org.au/

Bipolar Australia: https://www.bipolaraustralia.org.au/

Black Dog Institute: https://www.blackdoginstitute.org.au/

Headspace: https://headspace.org.au/eheadspace/

Lifeline: https://www.lifeline.org.au/

Medicare Mental Health: https://www.medicarementalhealth.gov.au/

Sane Australia: https://www.sane.org/

Suicide Callback Service: https://www.suicidecallbackservice.org.au/